GW00649725

ITIL® Practitioner Guidance

AXELOS.com

Published by TSO (The Stationery Office), part of Williams Lea,
and available from:

Online
www.tsoshop.co.uk

Mail, Telephone, Fax & E-mail
TSO
PO Box 29, Norwich, NR3 1GN
Telephone orders/General enquiries: 0333 202 5070
Fax orders: 0333 202 5080
E-mail: customer.services@tso.co.uk
Textphone 0333 202 5077

TSO@Blackwell and other Accredited Agents

Copyright © AXELOS Limited 2016

All rights reserved. No part of this publication may be reproduced in any form or by any means without permission in writing from AXELOS Limited.

Applications to reuse, reproduce or republish material in this publication should be sent to: The Licensing Team, AXELOS Limited, Rosebery Court, St Andrews Business Park, Norwich, Norfolk NR7 0HS. Email licensing@AXELOS.com

AXELOS, the AXELOS logo, the AXELOS swirl logo, ITIL®, MoP®, M_o_R®, MoV®, MSP®, P3M3®, P3O®, PRINCE2® and PRINCE2 Agile® are registered trade marks of AXELOS Limited.

RESILIA™ is a trade mark of AXELOS Limited.

Cover image © istock/Alkalyne

Chp 1 © istock/George Clerk; Chp 2 © istock/northlightimages; Chp 3 © istock/SINGTO2; Chp 4 © istock/TheYok; Chp 5 © istock/4FR; Chp 6 © istock/mddphoto; Chp 7 © istock/George Clerk

Image 5.1 © istock/pepifoto

Figure 6.1 reproduced by kind permission of ITSMF International Limited and Karen Ferris. J.P Kotter's eight steps for leading change, adapted, reprinted with permission from "Leading Change" by John. P Kotter. Harvard Business School Press, Boston 1995. Copyright 1995 by Harvard Business Publishing all rights reserved.

First published 2016

ISBN 9780113314874

Printed in the United Kingdom for The Stationery Office
Material is FSC certified and produced using ECF pulp, sourced from fully sustainable forests.
P002769918   01/16

Contents

List of figures

List of tables

Foreword

Every organization changes constantly. So many forces are in play – customer requirements, competitors' actions, changing markets, new legislation, the desire to reduce costs etc. – that new circumstances are constantly being created to which the organization must respond in order to survive.

Organizations that embrace change are in a strong position to achieve their goals. By accepting the fact that everything they do can be improved, they give themselves the opportunity to analyse their processes, their services and their products, and to work to improve them.

At AXELOS, we constantly apply that thinking to our portfolio of products. We always ask how they can be improved, developed and extended. The ITIL® Practitioner qualification and the accompanying guidance are a result of that process of continual improvement. They fill a gap in the portfolio that we learned of through listening to our community.

The qualification has been developed for ITSM professionals who have an understanding of the ITIL framework but who need advice on how to adopt and adapt it within their day-to-day work practices. By utilizing core skills such as metrics and measurement, communication, and organizational change management, by adhering to the guiding principles of ITSM, and by following the CSI approach, we believe that practitioners will have everything they need to take on the challenges of their profession.

Abid Ismail
CEO
AXELOS Global Best Practice

About AXELOS

AXELOS is a joint venture company created by the Cabinet Office on behalf of Her Majesty's Government in the United Kingdom and Capita plc to run the Global Best Practice portfolio. It boasts an enviable track record and an unmatched portfolio of products, including ITIL®, PRINCE2® and RESILIA™. RESILIA is the new Cyber Resilience Best Practice portfolio.

Used in the private, public and voluntary sectors in more than 180 countries worldwide, the Global Best Practice products have long been associated with achievement, heightened standards and truly measurable improved quality.

AXELOS has an ambitious programme of investment for developing innovative solutions and stimulating the growth of a vibrant and open international ecosystem of training, consultancy and examination organizations. Developments to the portfolio also include the launch of PRINCE2 Agile®, which is fully aligned with AXELOS Global Best Practice.

PUBLICATIONS

AXELOS publishes a comprehensive range of guidance, including:

- *ITIL® Service Strategy*
- *ITIL® Service Design*
- *ITIL® Service Transition*
- *ITIL® Service Operation*
- *ITIL® Continual Service Improvement*
- *PRINCE2 Agile®*
- *Managing Successful Projects with PRINCE2®*
- *Managing Successful Programmes* (MSP®)
- *Management of Portfolios* (MoP®)
- *Portfolio, Programme and Project Offices* (P3O®)
- *Management of Risk* (M_o_R®)
- *Management of Value* (MoV®)
- Portfolio, Programme and Project Management Maturity Model (P3M3®)
- *RESILIA™: Cyber Resilience Best Practice.*

Full details of the range of materials published under the AXELOS Global Best Practice banner, including *ITIL® Practitioner Guidance*, can be found at:

https://www.axelos.com/best-practice-solutions

If you would like to inform AXELOS of any changes that may be required to *ITIL® Practitioner Guidance* or any other AXELOS publication, please log them at:

https://www.axelos.com/best-practice-feedback

CONTACT INFORMATION

Full details on how to contact AXELOS can be found at:

https://www.axelos.com

For further information on qualifications and training accreditation, please visit:

https://www.axelos.com/qualifications

https://www.axelos.com/training-organization-benefits

For all other enquiries, please email:

Ask@AXELOS.com

Acknowledgements

AXELOS Ltd is grateful to everyone who has contributed to the development of this guidance and in particular would like to thank the following:

HEAD OF ITSM

Kaimar Karu (author)

Kaimar is the head of ITSM at AXELOS, leading the development of ITIL with a focus on providing value for both organizations and professionals, and showing how the combination of ITIL, DevOps and other frameworks and philosophies can deliver strong service management.

Kaimar is an experienced ITSM practitioner who has a career background in IT support, software development and project management. He has a passion for education and taught in schools and universities before becoming a trainer, delivering courses for professionals in both the private and the public sectors across Europe. In 2013, Kaimar was elected president of itSMF Estonia after serving as a board member for five consecutive years. He is now based in London but rarely seen there as he is on the road most of the time, working with practitioners around the world to ensure ITIL remains relevant and valuable.

PRACTITIONER ARCHITECT TEAM

Kevin Behr

Kevin brings more than 25 years of frontline experience in business management, technology and thought leadership to the team, having served as a chief information officer, chief technology officer, chief strategist and chief operations officer. In addition to his leadership roles in public and private companies, Kevin also co-founded the IT Process Institute with Gene Kim, and served as its president for the first five years. Kevin is the author of *The Definitive Guide to IT Management for the Adaptive Enterprise* (Hewlett-Packard) and *The Shortcut Guide to Managing Certificate Lifecycles* (Realtime–Thawte), as well as being co-author of *The Visible Ops Handbook* (IT Process Institute) and *The Phoenix Project: A Novel about IT, DevOps, and Helping your Business Win* (IT Revolution Press).

Karen Ferris (author)

A director of Macanta Consulting, Karen is an internationally acclaimed service management professional with a reputation for providing both strategic and practical advice on the implementation and maintenance of service management and organizational change management policies.

An internationally sought-after keynote speaker, in 2005 Karen won the President's Prize for Best Speaker at the Australian national conference of itSMF, while in 2007 she was awarded the inaugural Service Management Champion accolade by the same organization. In 2011, she authored the acclaimed itSMF publication, *Balanced Diversity – A Portfolio Approach to Organizational Change*, introducing a new framework to ensure that service management changes become embedded into the fabric of an organization.

In 2014, Karen was granted the itSMF Australia Lifetime Achievement award for her contribution to the industry.

Lou Hunnebeck (author)

An ITIL Expert with more than 30 years' experience in the service industries, Lou's passion for improving how we do what we do has led her to IT service management from a background of process consulting, training and service management consulting systems. Devoted to advancing the art and practice of service management, Lou is the author of *ITIL Service Design* (2011), is on the senior examination panel for ITIL, and speaks regularly at industry meetings to spread the message of ITSM best practice.

Barclay Rae (author)

Barclay is an experienced ITSM mentor and business manager. He has worked for a number of ITSM organizations and provides ITSM consultancy and media analysis services to the ITSM industry. He is currently the interim CEO for *it*SMF UK and is co-author of the certification standards for the Service Desk Institute (SDI).

Barclay is a regular speaker at industry conferences and events, including SITS (Strategic Information Technology Services), SDI, *it*SMF, Pink Elephant and UCISA (Universities and Colleges Information Systems Association). In 2014, he was voted ITSM's Contributor of the Year for SITS.

Barclay writes blogs, research articles and white papers on ITSM for a variety of industry organizations and vendors, and hosts the ITSMTV online TV channel. He is the creator of ITSM Goodness, a set of practical guidelines, tips and tools for successful ITSM.

Stuart Rance (author)

Stuart is a consultant, trainer and author, and owner of Optimal Service Management Ltd. Stuart works with a wide variety of clients in many countries, helping them to use ideas from ITSM and information security management to create business value for both themselves and their customers. He is a chartered fellow of the British Computer Society (FBCS CITP) and a certified information systems security professional (CISSP).

Stuart shares his expertise widely, regularly presenting at events and writing books, white papers, blogs and pocket guides on all aspects of IT. He is the author of *ITIL Service Transition* (2011) and co-author of *RESILIA: Cyber Resilience Best Practice* and the ITIL V3 Glossary. He has written many pocket guides for *it*SMF and for the official ITIL portfolio.

Paul Wilkinson

Paul has been involved in the IT industry for more than 25 years and has a broad background in IT operations, IT management and product innovation and development. He was project team lead in the original BITE (Business IT Excellence) process modelling of ITIL, an ITIL V2 author and a member of the ITIL V3 advisory group. He is co-owner of GamingWorks and co-developer of a range of business simulations focusing on ITSM, project management, business process management, business and IT alignment, and alliance management. He is co-author and developer of the ABC of ICT products and publications.

Paul is a recognized speaker at international ITSM and best-practice conferences and events. He has been actively engaged with thousands of customer organizations through his presentations, workshops, business game exercises and consulting engagements.

REVIEWERS

Aprill Allen, Knowledge Bird; Markus Bause, Serview; Alison Beadle, Learning Tree; Ole Christensen, Sopra Steria; Katie Copus, CSME; Barry Corless, Global Knowledge; Mauricio Corona, BP Gurus; Richard Dally, Unisys Ltd; Robert Den Broeder, Trigono; Troy DuMoulin, Pink; Nasser El-Hout, SMCE; Sofi Fahlberg, SIS Marine; Peter Farenden, Tanlan Training Ltd; Mark Flynn, APMG; Danilo Garci; Anastasia Gavana, PeopleCert; Vivek Joseph, PeopleCert; Dave Kelsey, BCS; Claudine Koers, Quint Wellington Redwood; Rick Lemieux, itSM Solutions LLC; Tricia Lewin, Matwin Management Services Ltd; Ruaidhri McSharry, SureSkills; Anita Myrberg, BITA Service Management; Jospeh Nduiu; Christian Feldbech Nissen, CFN People; Mark O'Loughlin, IT Alliance Group; Deryth Pearson, FOX IT; Oleg Skrynnik, Cleverics; Adam Stewart, QA; Mimi Struck, CSME; Connie Tai, IT Preneurs; Sharon Taylor, Aspect Group Inc; Loukia Tsagkli, PeopleCert; Bradley Utterback, HP Education Services; Dave Van Herpen, Sogeti; Martin Waters, QA.

1

Introduction

This chapter covers:

- Using ITIL – adopt and adapt
- Understanding service
- Delivery models
- Service management versus IT service management

1 Introduction

ITIL's best **practices** are based upon the practical experience of thousands of **organization**s from around the world. Anyone who adopts ITIL will benefit from many years of hard-earned knowledge. Adopting these practices in a highly effective and efficient way requires not only a sound understanding of ITIL best practices themselves, but also an understanding of the underlying concepts and principles. The **IT service management (ITSM)** professional who assimilates these key principles will be in a much better position to achieve maximum success in **service management**.

1.1 USING ITIL – ADOPT AND ADAPT

ITIL, as with any framework, methodology, body of knowledge or philosophy, is only as valuable as the results it helps to achieve. How the practices are applied is critical. It is necessary at all times to remember what is to be accomplished and why it needs to be accomplished. Following book examples or practices blindly, without considering their appropriateness to the situation, is a certain way to fail. ITIL is not an instruction manual.

How does a **service provider** ensure the organization has clearly defined **role**s and responsibilities, efficiently operated processes and a shared focus on providing services to **customer**s? The answer is that they adopt a service management approach and adapt the guidance provided in the ITIL publications to the specific needs and circumstances of their organization. Success requires the application of critical judgement on all occasions.

So, when using ITIL:

- **Adopt** Commit to adopting a service-oriented, customer-focused culture. Success in service management is based on a genuine commitment to this **change**. Evidence of such commitment can be seen, not in the way the people in an organization talk, but rather in the way in which they behave and in how those behaviours are incentivized.
- **Adapt** Strive to understand ITIL best practices, to understand why they are recommended, and then to apply critical thought to adapting those best practices to the organization's circumstances, needs, goals and **objective**s.

In the **process** of adopting and adapting, it is essential to remember that ITIL guidance is based on practices that have worked for a significant number of organizations around the world. That is why they have become recognized as best practices. But every organization is different. The needs of the organization should be the deciding factor in how the best practices are applied.

It is essential to start by fully understanding the practices that ITIL recommends and why they are recommended. After all, the reason that best practices can help organizations go further towards service excellence and to go there faster than they might have gone without them is because the organizations are benefiting from the trial and error of a large number of others in similar circumstances. If organizations do not understand the recommended practices well enough, then they cannot determine what can be effectively used in their own organization versus what needs to be either significantly modified or even ignored.

Once the ITIL guidance has been understood at a critical level, it is possible to successfully assess its **value** to a particular organization in the context of its **vision**, goals, objectives, circumstances and constraints. In this way, the most practical and appropriate approach can be defined and adopted, and real value can be delivered to customers and captured by the service provider.

1.2 UNDERSTANDING SERVICE

At the heart of ITIL and ITSM in general is the concept of **service**. Services are the focus of service providers and customers alike. ITSM professionals are dedicated to making the provision of service highly effective and highly efficient. However, success in this endeavour is dependent on a real understanding of the concept of service and how that concept will impact the activities of practitioners and the experience of the customer.

So let us start at the beginning. Practitioners must fully understand the key elements of ITIL's definition of a service in order to fully understand how to make the right contributions in the right way.

1.2.1 Service and the service provider

Definition: Service

A service is a means of delivering value to customers by facilitating outcomes that customers want to achieve without the ownership of specific costs and risks.

A service is about allowing a customer to get, do or have something that they want, without the customer needing to own and manage the individual elements necessary to obtain what they desire. Achieving their desired **outcome**s should be easy for the customer. Making it easy for the customer is the **mission** of the service provider.

Definition: Service provider

A service provider is an organization supplying services to one or more internal customers or external customers.

1.2.2 Customer

In each situation, the service provider must determine who the customer is. Who receives value from the service being delivered? Depending on the nature of the service provider, there may be customers at multiple levels.

Definition: Customer

A customer is someone who buys goods or services. The customer of an IT service provider is the person or group who defines and agrees the service level targets.

1.2.2.1 The customer for services

Let us begin by looking at this from the perspective of an internal IT department as IT service provider to an organization of which they are a part. Ultimately, the customers of the **business** itself are the ones who must receive value. The business does not receive revenue or other benefit from their customers unless those customers receive value from the business.

In this **internal service provider** model, from the perspective of the IT department, some **IT service**s may be utilized directly by external customers, making it easy to identify the contribution of these services to value creation for the external customer. But many IT services directly benefit only internal IT customers, in which case, the contribution of these services to value creation for external customers may be more difficult to trace. Understanding the **value network** is important to working out who is receiving value in this situation.

Definition: Value network

A value network is a complex set of relationships between two or more groups or organizations. Value is generated through exchange of knowledge, information, goods or services.

1.2.2.2 The customer for processes

For the purposes of adopting a service-oriented way of working, much attention will be paid not only to services, but also to the processes used to deliver those services. When working with processes, the concept of who benefits from the work of the process can be useful; in a way, we are determining who the customer of the process is. For a deeper discussion of this topic, see section 2.1.2.

1.2.3 Value

Definition: Value

The benefits delivered in proportion to the resources put into acquiring them. The value of a service comes from what it enables someone to do. Services contribute value to an organization only when their value is perceived to be higher than the cost of obtaining the service.

In the definition of value, the 'someone' referred to is the customer. Putting this together leads us to the following three questions when considering the value of a service:

● What service will be provided to the customer?
● What will the customer be able to achieve through the use of the service?
● How much will the service cost the customer?

For planning purposes, the questions are posed in the future tense – will be. For historical analysis purposes, the questions should be posed in the past tense – were, did. Because services must deliver value to customers, only the customer can decide whether or not they receive value from a service.

1.2.3.1 Sources of value

When working to ensure that a service delivers value, we must remember that the value comes not only from the functionality of the service – its **utility**, or fitness for purpose – but also from how well that utility is working – its **warranty**, or fitness for use (see *ITIL Service Strategy*, section 2.1.6). The most desirable functionality is useless if it is not delivered at levels that meet the needs of the customer.

1.2.3.2 Applying the concept

The **impact** of this concept of value on the work of practitioners should be powerful and ubiquitous. Whether working on designing a new service, improving an existing one, rolling out a new process or improving an existing one, ITSM professionals must consider how the work will either directly or indirectly support the delivery of value to the customers.

By understanding the manner in which an ITSM adoption action will deliver value to the business or customer, practitioners gain the ability to focus their efforts more appropriately. Additionally, they may be more successful in gaining support (and perhaps funding) for their service improvements by demonstrating the value associated with the effort.

Example

Consider an IT service provider that is concerned about a high percentage of repeats of the same incident. Staff members involved in incident management may feel that they are wasting a great deal of time responding to the same kind of incident over and over again.

If the organization is able to implement an effective problem management process that identifies the root causes of these repetitive incidents and drives permanent elimination of the problems, then instances of the repeat incidents should stop occurring, or at least should be dramatically reduced. Incident management staff will benefit directly from this process improvement, as they will no longer have to spend time resolving these incidents. However, and more importantly, the business will benefit because the end-users who were experiencing the service disruption from these incidents will no longer be disrupted. The services on which the end-users depend will have been made more stable.

Essentially, service warranty will have improved because of a process improvement.

1.2.4 Outcomes

Definition: Outcome

An outcome is the result of carrying out an activity, following a process, or delivering an IT service etc. The term is used to refer to intended results as well as actual results.

When the customer or business can do the things that allow them to meet their objectives, then the outcomes are more likely to be achieved.

1.2.4.1 Outcomes versus outputs

Definition: Output

An output is a specialist product (the tangible or intangible artefact) that is produced, constructed or created as a result of a planned activity and handed over to a user(s).

Outcomes are different from mere **outputs**. One output of a wedding organizing service may be completed contracts with wedding **suppliers**, but the outcome the customer expects is a wedding that fulfils the dreams of the bride and groom while staying within their **budget** and on schedule. A **change management** process may produce an output of reports or **metrics**, but those are not the outcomes desired by the customer. The customer expects sound change management to deliver to them the ability to benefit from appropriate changes while still experiencing stable services with minimal unplanned interruptions.

If a service provider focuses on outputs only and either neglects or fails to understand the customer's desired outcomes, the service provided may not have delivered value to the customer.

1.2.4.2 Understanding desired outcomes

Often in a customer/service provider relationship, it can be difficult for the service provider to completely understand the outcomes the customer truly wants. Some customers do not express themselves in terms that are meaningful to the service provider. It is the job of the service provider to learn to understand the customer, not the other way around.

Many customers, in an effort to be clear about what they want, actually try to design the details of the service themselves.

Example

Consider a situation in which a sales department wants to encourage its sales force to move away from their desks and get out into the field. The director of sales imagines a mobile app which would allow sales people to do more work remotely.

What the service provider needs to know is, not the solution the director imagined, but what outcomes are needed. In the end, the desired outcomes relate to the ability for sales people to perform various functions in the field that they currently do from the office. The service provider may not need to write something new, but may be able to leverage existing options on the market. If the service provider focuses on the real desired outcomes, then they can apply their specialized capabilities to the real task at hand.

It is also important for the service provider to remember that part of the customer's required outcomes relate to **cost** and schedule. If the customer had unlimited time and/or money, they might define a much longer list of **requirement**s, but in reality no customer is without limits in these areas. When a balance needs to be struck between **function**, cost and schedule, going back to the core outcomes that the customer or business truly needs can help to control the scope while still delivering a solution that satisfies the customer. The customer is the expert in what success looks like to them. The service provider brings the expertise on what is possible, at what cost and within what timeframe. By focusing on outcomes, the customer and service provider can work together to bring these perspectives into a balance that meets the needs of the customer and/or business.

The art of being a superior service provider is in not being a mere order-taker, but in being able to draw out from the customer their genuine needs and desires. What would success look like to them? Then the service provider can apply their expertise and creativity to the delivery of those outcomes.

1.2.5 Costs

Definition: Cost

A cost is the amount of money spent on a specific activity, IT service or business unit. Costs consist of real cost (money), notional cost (e.g. people's time) and depreciation.

In the context of the definition of a service, cost comes into play in two key ways:

● **Overall price** The customer wants to know how much it will cost them to achieve the outcomes they desire (and they are willing to pay for).

● **Individual costs** The materials, time, work, etc. necessary to deliver the service – and therefore the outcomes – are not free; there is a cost to each.

1.2.5.1 Making things easier for the customer

If the customer had to do all the work associated with achieving their desired outcomes by themselves, without the assistance of a service provider, they would need to concern themselves with each of the individual costs. The customer would have to investigate all the possibilities and cost them out, create and maintain relationships with the providers of the required service components, obtain the components at the right price, and so forth. That is a great deal of work. And because the customer may not have expertise in many of the individual areas involved, the process may result in many costly mistakes.

This brings us back to the nature of a service and how a service makes things easier for the customer. In a service provider/customer relationship, the service provider takes over responsibility for all or most of the individual costs, presenting an overall cost or price to the customer for their consideration. Without the burden of concerning themselves with every detail, the customer is then free to decide if the outcomes associated with the service are worth the price of achieving them. If the customer thinks the equation works for them, then they will feel they are receiving value.

1.2.5.2 Complexities in addressing cost

Outcome weighed against price might seem an easy equation to evaluate, but it is rarely that simple.

For the service provider to accurately estimate the total cost – and from it, the price – of delivering the service, they have to clearly understand what will satisfy the customer, fully comprehend what will go into producing and delivering the service, and accurately estimate the effort required to do the work. When the customer asks if something new is possible, service providers frequently answer the question from a purely technical perspective, without advising the customer of the related impact to the budget and schedule. Working closely with the customer to manage requirements, and being transparent with the customer about the financial and schedule impacts of scope changes, will allow a reasonable balance to be maintained. Using an iterative approach when designing new or improved services can assist in managing the scope in a more flexible and responsive way.

Another important element of cost is accurately calculating the ongoing **operational cost**s of delivering a service. In many cases, the conversation between the service provider and customer focuses on the cost of turning the service on and does not adequately consider the subsequent ongoing costs. The cost of consistently delivering agreed levels of service over time needs to be defined, communicated and agreed.

1.2.6 Risks

Definition: Risk

A risk is a possible event that could cause harm or loss, or affect the ability to achieve objectives (see glossary for a full definition).

In its purest state, **risk** is uncertainty of outcome. In relation to a service, the customer wants to have confidence that, if they pay the price the service provider is asking for the service, the customer will actually achieve the promised outcomes. In order to appropriately manage the risks to service, the service provider must understand where the uncertainties lie, understand the degree of each kind of uncertainty, and the cost of lowering risk.

1.2.6.1 Making things easier for the customer

As with costs, if the customer did not engage a service provider, the customer would have to take direct responsibility for all the individual risks associated with achieving their outcomes. What if one of the suppliers does not deliver on time? What if the first build does not work? What if the user interface is too difficult to use? What if the real costs are significantly higher than the amount budgeted for?

Once again, in a service provider/customer relationship, the service provider takes over the responsibilities for the risks at the detailed level, leaving primarily the broad scope risks for the customer. The service provider makes it their business to manage the detailed level of risk on behalf of the customer, based on what matters most to that customer. The customer contributes to the reduction of risk through activities such as:

● actively participating in the definition of requirements and the clarification of required outcomes

● clearly communicating to the service provider the critical success factors (CSFs) and constraints the customer believes apply to the activity/service

● ensuring the service provider has access to the appropriate customer staff to maintain alignment throughout the initiative and ongoing service delivery.

1.2.6.2 Collaborating with the customer

When in doubt, the service provider must work with the customer to provide clear information about choices and to understand which risks the customer is willing to accept and which ones they are not.

Example

Consider a situation in which the customer needs to implement new functionality in a key business service in order to be in compliance with new government regulations. If the functionality is not in place by a particular date, a large fine will be levied against the company. At the same time, the customer keeps bringing up additional functionality that they would very much like to have.

If including all the desired functionality creates a significant risk that there will be insufficient time left to fully test the changes before the deadline, the service provider must discuss the situation with the customer and advise them of the choice that faces them. They could include all the functionality, but risk the service failing on deployment. Or they could narrow the focus to what is required by the new legislation and increase the likelihood of a successful deployment.

Only the customer can decide what risks they are willing to accept, but the service provider is responsible for making the nature and scope of the risks clear, and proceeding based on the customer's wishes.

1.2.6.3 Risks for the service provider

Customers cannot benefit from a service if the service provider becomes unable to provide it. Service providers must carefully evaluate the risk of offering each service.

Example

Consider a service provider that has a service that is very expensive to deliver and depends upon a single supplier for a key component. Because of the cost of delivering the service compared to the price that customers are willing to pay for it, the service provider does not make very much profit on the service.

If the supplier increases their prices to the service provider, then the price of the service to the customer may become prohibitive. If the supplier goes out of business, the service provider will not be able to deliver the service at all, regardless of price.

These represent risks for the service provider. It is possible that the service provider may decide that they are not willing to offer this service any longer. This is particularly likely if they are an external service provider, selling their services on the open market.

1.2.7 Putting it all together

ITSM professionals need to keep the definition of a service and the components of that definition clearly in mind as they work to adopt a service-oriented approach in their work and to improve both **efficiency** and **effectiveness**.

Clearly identify who the customer is. Then, for each situation, consider the four components of the definition of a service:

● **Value** How will the service, process, partner, etc. help to deliver value to the customer?
● **Outcomes** What are the specific outcomes required by the customer that the service will facilitate?
● **Costs** What are the true and complete costs associated with achieving the outcomes?
● **Risk** What are the risks that, if they materialize, could endanger the achievement of the outcomes?

The four components of the definition of a service should be carefully evaluated in relation to each other and in relation to the needs of the customer in order to support good decision-making. Finally, decisions must always be made with full awareness of the larger context, such as overall budgets for all services, balancing the needs of all customers – even when those needs seem to conflict – and, in the context of the overall vision, goals and objectives of the customer and/or business.

If practitioners ensure they are addressing value, outcomes, costs and risks (VOCR) in the service of their customer, they are more likely to have satisfied customers and a thriving service provider organization.

1.2.8 Service management

Definition: Service management

Service management is a set of specialized organizational capabilities for providing value to customers in the form of services.

This definition of service management (further explored in *ITIL Service Strategy*, section 2.1.2) is also helpful to ITSM professionals, as it can help them to focus on the most important actions when adopting a service-oriented approach. The central takeaway from this definition is that, in order to deliver value to the customer via their services, the IT service provider must not only rely on the skills of individuals, but must also develop organizational capabilities.

It is not enough to have a group of talented, highly motivated individual staff members. The staff members and teams within the service provider need to truly collaborate. This includes smooth integration and coordination with external suppliers who are contributing to the provision of the service. Through clearly defined roles and responsibilities, efficiently operating shared processes, and a shared focus on providing service to customers, the IT service provider dramatically improves their ability to allow the customer to benefit from the service provider's specialized skills. Customers are not obliged to become experts in what the service provider knows, but can rather leverage the service provider's capabilities to achieve their own goals and objectives.

1.2.8.1 Ensuring efficiency and balance

When discussing organizational capabilities, it is important to remember that one of the most valuable is the ability to adapt and evolve. Many organizations misconstrue ITIL's emphasis on process as meaning we must institute rigid controls that never vary. In fact, many people are passionately opposed to process because they see the word as synonymous with bureaucracy. Nothing could be further from the truth. Good process includes only those controls that are absolutely necessary for the consistent achievement of the desired results.

Good process should include regular checks on the fitness for purpose and fitness for use of the process in context, and on the application of appropriate corrections and/or improvements. Some organizations need more structure and control, while other organizations work well when they are highly fluid, evolving and adapting their ways of working on a much more frequent basis. Striking the appropriate balance between control and chaos is one of those organizational capabilities we are talking about.

1.2.8.2 Service integration and management

Service integration and management (SIAM) is a service **capability** and set of practices in a **model** and approach that enables an organization to manage multiple service providers in a consistent and efficient way such that the resulting goods and services meet customer needs. SIAM is not a process; it builds on, elaborates and complements the ITIL framework.

Effective SIAM seeks to combine the benefits of best-of-breed-based multi-sourcing of services with the simplicity of single sourcing, minimizing the risks inherent in multi-sourced approaches and masking the **supply chain** complexity from the consumers of the services.

1.3 DELIVERY MODELS

When an organization truly embraces the idea of being a service provider, the character of everything they do will undergo a shift from using a technology delivery model to adopting a service provider model.

1.3.1 Technology delivery model

A technology delivery model is characterized by the focus on efficient delivery and management of individual technical components and/or systems. In this model, the delivering organization typically functions as an order-taker, frequently involving the customer directly in technological matters such as server and storage decisions. Within IT, teams work in a silo-oriented manner, each one functioning in partial isolation without much inter-team coordination. The focus is on installation, maintenance, upgrading, preventing failures etc.

1.3.2 Service provider model

By contrast, a service provider model is characterized by the holistic management of fit-for-purpose and fit-for-use services. The service provider uses shared processes to allow the internal teams to work together to deliver not just technology, but actual outcomes to the customer. The service provider exerts significant effort in understanding the customer's desired outcomes – what is of value to them – and insulates the customer from having to take responsibility for all the individual associated costs and risks. The focus is on delivering results and making things easier for the customer – that is, a service-oriented approach.

1.3.3 Contrasting the models

The contrast between these models is easy to see in a traditional internal IT service provider environment, but it is equally relevant to external service providers.

> ### Example
>
> A service provider may use highly technical terminology to discuss issues with the customer, sharing more detail than the customer either cares about or can understand. This could confuse the customer and make them feel that they must have the same level of expertise as the service provider just to work with them.
>
> If the service provider, however, focuses on outcomes and on creating a complete service experience, providing key information to the customer in easy-to-understand language and managing the details behind the scenes, the customer is more likely to feel they are being ably served. If the customer requests more technical detail, the service provider can deliver it, but that is for the customer to determine. It should not be the default position of the service provider.

The work to make the shift from a primarily technology delivery model to the adoption of a service-oriented approach occurs at all levels of a service provider organization. Everyone contributes to making it happen.

1.4 SERVICE MANAGEMENT VERSUS IT SERVICE MANAGEMENT

The guidance documented in ITIL was originally designed for IT service providers, with a particular emphasis on internal IT departments providing services to the organizations of which they are a part. The current version of the guidance, while starting with that same perspective, is nevertheless applicable in a much broader context. The core principles of service and services, value, outcomes, costs and risks are relevant to all kinds of service providers, not just those delivering IT services.

Regardless of what kind of service provider is using the ITIL guidance, it is important to note that the guidance is written for the service provider and is from the service provider's point of view, while still focusing on the value delivered to their customers. The intent of the guidance is to assist service providers in becoming more successful in delivering value.

2

Guiding principles

This chapter covers:

- Focus on value
- Design for experience
- Start where you are
- Work holistically
- Progress iteratively
- Observe directly
- Be transparent
- Collaborate
- Keep it simple
- Applying the guiding principles

2 Guiding principles

The journey to adopt a service-oriented approach to IT, as embodied in IT service management (ITSM), is not a matter of installing software or changing the design of the infrastructure. At the heart of ITSM is a powerful cultural shift from focusing on technology to focusing on services. This means concerning ourselves with the outcomes that technology must enable for the customer, how that will deliver value, and dedicating the service provider to continual improvement.

Successful adoption of this new mind-set will be more likely if all aspects of the effort are guided by the principles outlined here. These guiding principles distil the core messages of ITIL specifically and ITSM in general, facilitating improvement activities of all types and at all levels. They are the 'how' that can guide organizations in their work as they adopt a service management approach and adapt the guidance provided in the ITIL publications to their own specific needs and circumstances.

These guiding principles are also reflected in many of the other frameworks, methods, standards, philosophies and/or bodies of knowledge that may be used in an organization, such as Lean, agile, DevOps and others, allowing organizations to effectively integrate the use of multiple ways of working into an overall approach to providing services.

Tip

This publication makes extensive use of the word 'improvement', which might imply that these guiding principles are not intended for use when a new ITSM adoption programme is being undertaken or a new service or process is being introduced. Nothing could be further from the truth. Even a brand new ITSM adoption programme is an effort to improve not only what is being done, but also how it is being done, and these guiding principles apply. Whether working on something seen as truly new or changing something in existence, consider the work as covered by the term 'improvement'.

The guiding principles described in Table 2.1 should be referenced throughout all improvement activities, whether **strategic**, tactical or operational in nature, whether undertaken by a large group, a small team or even an individual. These guiding principles are also applicable to any type of service provider model, whether internal, external or shared services, and any type of service provider, whether IT or non-IT.

2.1 FOCUS ON VALUE

Everything the service provider does needs to map back, directly or indirectly, to value for their customer. This is one of the most fundamental principles found throughout ITIL and ITSM. The customer could be a person, a group, the whole organization or a combination, depending on what the service is and who the service provider is.

ITIL Service Strategy says that 'the value of a service comes from what it enables someone to do' and defines the characteristics of value as:

● Defined by the customer
● Affordable mix of features
● Achievement of objectives
● Changing over time and circumstances.

Value can come in many forms, such as increased productivity, reduced pain, reduced costs, the ability to pursue new markets, better competitive position etc. A service can deliver value to a customer only if it has utility (is **fit for purpose**) and warranty (is **fit for use**), all from the perspective of what matters to the customer (for more information, see *ITIL Service Strategy*, section 2.1.6 and Figure 2.2).

Table 2.1 Overview of guiding principles

Principle	Description
Focus on value	Everything the service provider does needs to map, directly or indirectly, to value for the customer and/or the organization. This is one of the most fundamental principles of ITIL and ITSM. It is the customer who determines what is of value to them, not the service provider. Continual improvement must be focused around making improvements that will result in greater value being delivered to the customer.
Design for experience	It is critical to retain the focus not only on business/customer value, but also on the experience that both customers and **user**s have when they interact with the service or service provider. This is frequently called the 'customer experience' and it must be actively managed.
Start where you are	Resist the temptation to start from scratch and build something new without considering what is already available to be leveraged. Based on the vision for the future and how that will deliver value to the customer, there is likely to be a great deal in the current services, processes, programmes, projects, people etc. that can be used to create that future.
Work holistically	No service or component stands alone. The results delivered to the organization or customer will suffer unless the service provider works on the whole, not just on the parts. Results are delivered to the customer through the effective and efficient management of a complex integration of hardware, software, data, processes, architectures, metrics, tools, people and partners, all coordinated to provide a defined value.
Progress iteratively	Even huge initiatives have to be accomplished iteratively. Resist the temptation to do everything at once. By organizing work into smaller, manageable sections that can be executed and completed in a timely manner, the focus on each smaller improvement is sharper and easier to maintain. Improvement iterations can be sequential or simultaneous, based on dependencies or lack thereof. The key is for each individual improvement to be manageable and managed, to ensure that real results are returned in a timely manner and built upon to create more improvement.
Observe directly	To know what is really going on, measure and/or observe it directly. Be sure to base decisions on information that is as accurate as it can be. Going to the source allows a reduction in the use of assumptions which, if proved unfounded, can be disastrous to timelines, budgets and the **quality** of results.
Be transparent	The more that people are aware of what is happening and why it is happening, then the more that people will help and fewer people will obstruct. Make things as transparent as possible.
Collaborate	When the right people are involved in the right ways, improvements benefit from better buy-in, better relevance (because better information is available for decision-making) and better likelihood of long-term success.
Keep it simple	If a process, service, action, metric etc. provides no value or produces no useful outcome, then eliminate it. In a process or procedure, use the minimum number of steps needed to accomplish the objective(s). Although this principle may seem obvious, it is frequently ignored, resulting in overly complex work methods that rarely maximize outcomes or minimize cost.

An IT department, or any service provider for that matter, can no longer treat the rest of the organization as something separate from itself. By the same token, service providers can no longer behave as simple order-takers. A service provider must first and foremost recognize that they are not providing hardware and software; they are providing value in the form of technology-based services that make it possible for the customer to achieve their goals. This means that the service provider, to understand what is of value to the customer or customer organization, must get to know the customer at a level of intimacy that many service providers avoid.

Central to this principle is the fact that it is the customer who determines what is of value, not the service provider. The service provider must, therefore, determine who the customer is in each situation. Who receives value from what is being delivered or improved? For a service, this should already have been defined. If not, it must be determined. For a process, this can be more challenging, but the impact that the process has on the services that are being delivered is the place to start.

Continual improvement must be focused around making improvements that will result in greater value being delivered to the customer.

2.1.1 The customer for services

From the perspective of the IT department, in what ITIL calls an internal service provider model, there are **internal customer**s (other departments in the organization) who are also integral to serving the external customers (the customers of the organization itself).

Some of the services the IT department provides will be used by internal customers (e.g. a service used by the human resources department for managing information about the company's employees), while other services may be used by external customers (e.g. an online banking service used by external clients of a retail bank).

The contribution of the services used by external customers to value creation for the business is direct. The contribution of the internal services to value creation for the business is more indirect.

Customers, services and value are discussed in section 3.2 of *ITIL Service Strategy*.

2.1.2 The customer for processes

When working with processes, the concept of who benefits from the work of the process can be useful. In a way, we are determining who the customer of the process is. Determining who needs to receive value from a process should include awareness of two perspectives:

● Every process delivers its primary results to a customer or **stakeholder** (see *ITIL Service Strategy*, section 2.2.2)

● The work of a process contributes, either directly or indirectly, to the delivery of one or more services.

Improvements to a process, therefore, should deliver better results for those who directly benefit from the process, as well as allowing the process to more successfully contribute to the related services.

Example

Consider a change management process that has good procedures for normal changes, but does not make much use of standard changes with the associated predefined controls and authorizations. Even though infrastructure standards and policies are in place, most infrastructure changes still have to follow the normal change procedures.

If the change management process is improved through the conversion of a significant number of normal infrastructure changes into standard changes (usually allowing for a significant proportion of these to be automated), the team members who manage the infrastructure will experience direct value in the form of the ability to work more rapidly and more simply. But these process improvements will also indirectly benefit the end customers in that they can make use of service improvements that depend on infrastructure changes more rapidly and with less disruption.

2.1.3 Value and improvement

Whether guiding an entire ITSM adoption programme or a single improvement by one staff member, the principle of focusing on value emphasizes the need for the improvement to result in more value for the customer. This principle is critical as a guide to achieving excellence in service provision, whatever frameworks or methodologies the organization is using. In fact, a focus on providing value to the customer is also central to many well-regarded methods, including both Lean and value chain mapping.

2.2 DESIGN FOR EXPERIENCE

As an organization adopts a service-oriented approach, it is critical to retain the focus not only on business/ customer value, but also on the end-to-end experience that both customers and users have when they interact with the service provider.

Often, we talk about this in terms of customer experience (CX), which has been described as:

> *'The entirety of the interactions a customer has with a company and its products. Understanding the customer experience is an integral part of customer relationship management. The overall experience reflects how the customer feels about the company and its offerings'* (http://www.businessdictionary.com/definition/customer-experience).

Note, however, that in this guidance, CX will be used to refer to both the experience of what ITIL calls the 'customer' and also the experience of what ITIL calls the 'user'.

2.2.1 The two sides of the customer experience

CX is both objective and subjective. For example, when a customer orders a product and receives what they ordered at the promised price in the promised delivery time, this aspect of their experience is objectively measurable. If during the purchase journey the customer feels that the ordering website did not have a professional look, this is subjective; it is a matter of opinion on the customer's part.

Failing to attend to both aspects of CX, particularly the subjective, will likely result in loss of confidence and support by those being served, and potentially the loss of their business entirely. Addressing the subjective side is the heart of managing CX, but it must be done with a full awareness of the objective side.

Organizations seek to understand and manage CX, not out of a sense of altruism, but rather because they see this as something that provides insight into areas that can positively impact profitability and/or business **performance.**

2.2.2 Moments of truth and designing for experience

Many organizations attempt to address improvements to CX by segmenting the customer's journey into 'touchpoints' (each time a customer or potential customer comes in contact with the brand before, during or after a purchase) or 'moments of truth' (touchpoints that give the customer the opportunity to form or change an opinion about the brand). This approach, however, can be very misleading as it frequently fails to uncover the real issues. After all, a customer may be satisfied with an individual interaction with the service provider, but still have an overall negative experience.

From a conceptual standpoint, every touchpoint is potentially a moment of truth and the service provider should look at all of them to view CX holistically, to see the entire flow collectively. From a practical standpoint, however, the service provider needs to have a place to start. It is important to prioritize. The service provider should begin by identifying those touchpoints that are having the greatest negative impact on the overall CX and address those first. These are the current moments of truth. Along the way, the service provider should continually monitor CX to validate that the overall experience is improving. As time goes on, the service provider can continue to work iteratively to address the touchpoints where the need for improvement is less obvious, gradually achieving the desired cumulative effect on the whole experience.

Only a comprehensive view of the end-to-end CX will uncover the real customer view.

2.2.3 Customer experience and process design

The principle of understanding CX is not dissimilar to the work of ITIL's **business relationship management** process, in which it is paramount to understand the business, the customer and their needs. The work of designing for CX should be a natural activity that is included not only when designing products and services, but also when designing processes. For a service provider, putting themselves in the position of the customer should become second nature, concerning themselves not only with interactions at the operational level, but also with addressing the end-to-end experience at the tactical and strategic levels.

Definition: Business relationship management

The process responsible for maintaining a positive relationship with customers. Business relationship management identifies customer needs and ensures that the service provider is able to meet these needs with an appropriate catalogue of services. This process has strong links with service level management.

2.2.4 Measuring the customer experience

CX, if measured effectively, should provide information that will have a tangible impact on the factors that the organization uses to judge success. In many organizations, the key factor used to judge corporate success is profitability, but the contribution of CX to success also applies to other organizations, such as those in the not-for-profit sector.

When designing for experience, it is wise to build in methods to measure the experience at the point where it occurs. For example, some airports measure the experience of going through security by placing a device at the passenger exit that has an interface with an array of smiley face buttons. As they pass by, the passenger simply presses the button with the smiley face that best represents their experience. This, combined with other metrics, can provide the understanding required in order to effect positive change.

2.3 START WHERE YOU ARE

In the excitement of eliminating old, unsuccessful methods and/or services and creating something better, there can be great temptation to start from scratch – to rip out what has been done in the past and build something completely new. But that is rarely necessary or wise. The start-over approach can be extremely wasteful, not only in terms of time, but also in terms of existing services, processes, people, tools etc. that could have significant value in the improvement effort. Do not start over without considering what is already available to be leveraged.

To apply this principle successfully:

- **Look at what exists as objectively as possible** Are the elements of the current state fit for use and fit for purpose? There is likely to be a great deal in the current services, processes, projects, people etc. that can be used to create the desired future state, provided the people making this judgement can be objective. It is sometimes the case that, because the current state is perceived to be extremely painful, people have difficulty looking at the situation in an unbiased way. Objective current-state assessment (the second step in the continual service improvement (CSI) approach) should uncover candidates for reuse.

- **When examples of successful practices or services are found in the current state, determine if and how these can be replicated or expanded upon to achieve the desired state** In many, if not most cases, leveraging what already exists will reduce the amount of work needed to transition from the current state to the desired state.

- **Apply your risk management skills** There are risks associated with reusing existing processes etc. (such as people continuing old behaviours in their entirety without being able to change at all) and risks associated with instituting something new (such as people not performing new procedures correctly). These risks should be weighed as part of the decision-making process.

- **Recognize that, very occasionally, nothing from the current state can be reused** Regardless of how desirable it may be to reuse, repurpose and recycle or even upcycle, there will be times when the only way to achieve the desired result is to start over. For example, for a sufficiently intransigent issue, it may be decided that the only way to make real change is to start with a clean slate, perhaps to make the determination to change clear to staff members in a dramatic way. Remember, however, that these situations are very, very rare.

2.3.1 Aligning with existing initiatives

If a person or team discovers an existing initiative with which their improvement work could align, it should be leveraged. It can be very wasteful to have multiple work streams that are attempting to do the same thing. Sometimes initiatives that could be complementary end up in conflict simply because they are not properly coordinated.

Successfully leveraging what already exists while still creating the desired new state will, to a great degree, be dependent on the success of the **organizational change management** (OCM) programme (for more information, see Chapter 6). The human factor is critical to change of any kind. OCM activities can help staff members to understand what is changing, how what is old is evolving and why they should embrace the new. Reinforcing what is working, improving what has potential, and eliminating only what truly does not fit with the desired new state will allow more iterative improvement, reduce resistance to change and reduce waste as the new state is achieved.

2.4 WORK HOLISTICALLY

No service, process, department or supplier stands alone. Results are delivered to the customer and/or business via the effective and efficient management of a complex integration of hardware, software, data, processes, architectures, metrics, tools, people and partners, all coordinated to provide a defined value.

The results delivered to the customer will suffer unless the service provider works on the whole, not just on the parts. In a complex system, the alteration of one element will impact others and these impacts need to be identified where possible, understood and factored into the **plan**.

Examples of this abound. In a restaurant, a change in the availability of a single ingredient may cause changes to menus, cooking processes, which dishes and kitchen equipment are used, the systems waiters use to enter orders from the dining room, etc. There may be negative impacts on the waiters' enthusiasm for selling the available menu and on the overall experience of the diners.

2.4.1 Specialization versus coordination

When dealing with services, whether an element is technical or non-technical, each part of the service and its impact on the overall results delivered must be considered. Achieving this holistic approach requires a balance between specialization and coordination. Because no one person or even one team can know everything about every subject or perform every required task, we need specialists who develop deep expertise in a specific area. Specialization is usually reflected in the organization of people with similar skills and responsibilities into teams or groups (known as 'functions' in ITIL).

But specialists must collaborate across boundaries and their work must be effectively and efficiently coordinated to allow the required overall results to be delivered. This coordination and collaboration is facilitated by shared processes. In this way, we see that working holistically is dependent on other guiding principles such as Collaborate.

The specialization provided by functions and the coordination enabled by shared processes are both essential in the lifecycle approach. Shared processes mitigate the risk of functions becoming isolated and disconnected from broader customer-focused outcomes. Mature functions provide critical competencies needed for process success.

2.4.2 Other reflections on working holistically

Figure 2.1 shows 'the four Ps' – people, processes, products, partners – which contribute to comprehensive and integrated service design. This is an expression in ITIL of the principle of working holistically. Addressing only one or two of the four Ps will not produce a service that is both fit for purpose and fit for use.

Another approach that can be helpful when working holistically is using what is known as the 'theory of constraints' (Goldratt and Cox, 1992) to identify bottlenecks in the end-to-end process. Looking at a service (or even the **service lifecycle** itself) from multiple perspectives is to recognize it as a group of interacting and interdependent elements forming a unified whole. This holistic approach is sometimes called 'systems

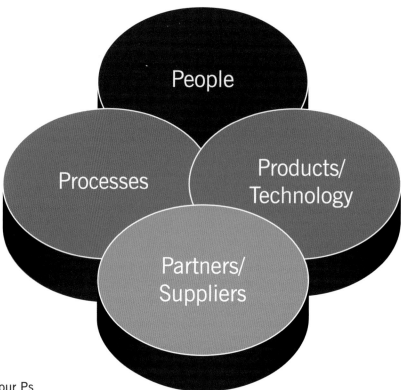

Figure 2.1 ITIL's four Ps

thinking'. By seeking to understand the system's structure, interdependencies and how changes in any area might affect the other parts and the whole system over time, organizations can create a sustainable long-term approach to service management. When systems can organically adapt to changes as they occur, the systems will be able to evolve in a way that is appropriate to the need.

2.5 PROGRESS ITERATIVELY

Each improvement undertaken should have a focused objective and scope that will allow it to be effectively and efficiently completed. An individual improvement may stand on its own but, most often, initiatives have to be accomplished iteratively. By organizing work into smaller, manageable sections that can be executed and completed in a timely manner, the focus on each smaller improvement is sharper and easier to maintain.

2.5.1 Timing improvement iterations

Improvement iterations can be sequential or simultaneous, based on dependencies or lack thereof. To effectively manage the work, a major improvement initiative or programme may be organized into several significant improvement initiatives, and each of these significant improvement initiatives may, in turn, have smaller improvement efforts within them. All of the initiatives, whatever the scope, will follow the same high-level steps.

For example, if the steps being followed are based on the Deming Plan-Do-Check-Act (PDCA) cycle, then Figure 2.2 demonstrates how smaller improvements may follow the same flow as those of which they are a part, while other improvements may be ongoing at the same time.

The key is for each individual improvement to be manageable in scope, managed to ensure that real results are returned in a timely manner, and built upon to create more improvement. The completion of each individual improvement allows progress to be shown, increasing confidence in the overall effort and allowing participants to feel a sense of accomplishment, even when the long-term goals may seem very far away.

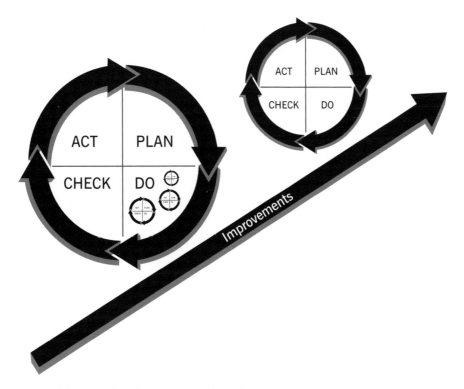

Figure 2.2 Related and independent improvement iterations

2.5.2 Scoping improvement iterations

How should each of the smallest improvement iterations be scoped? The easiest and most practical way of looking at this is to remember that the purpose of iteration is to accomplish something that is of value. It may be practical to follow the spirit of the concept known as minimum viable product (MVP), a term coined by Frank Robinson and often associated with Lean (see also Blank, 2010). In the context of software development or improvement, this can be understood as the smallest thing you can build that will still deliver value to the customer. The MVP must include everything necessary for the customer to receive that value, including testing, training, associated communication etc.

In the context of improvements like changes to a process, MVP can be understood as the smallest increment of improvement that delivers a **SMART** (specific, measurable, achievable, relevant and time-bound) objective (see *ITIL Service Strategy*, section 4.1.5.6). Just as with software or service MVPs, the scope of process improvements must include all the elements that will make the process improvement work, such as documentation and training staff members on the new approach. It is important to remember that the MVP needs to support learning from experience, so that the next iteration can be more successful.

In order for each improvement iteration to be successfully accomplished, it is important that the number of iterations in progress at any one time should be kept to a practical level – only start the quantity of things that can actually be finished. This principle, frequently described as 'limiting work in progress', is central to Kanban.

2.5.3 Other reflections on progressing iteratively

A commitment to an iterative approach is not only important when using the guidance in ITIL, it is also central to the agile methodology and the use of Scrum techniques, as well as being important to DevOps and PRINCE2 Agile. In all of these cases, the method or technique in question advocates working in small, manageable increments, each time producing some new state that is of value to the customer.

OBSERVE DIRECTLY

...ow what is really going on, measure and/or observe it directly. Be sure that decisions are based on ...mation that is as accurate as it can be. Observing directly (going to the source or the 'Gemba' as it is described in Lean) means actually going to the place where value-creating activity is occurring in the organization and seeing what really happens. What happens when a user calls the service desk? What happens in the store when a potential buyer comes in?

2.6.1 The role of measurement

Measurement can be included in this principle, but it should support the analysis of what was observed rather than replace it. Although it is true that some things can only be understood through observing and measuring their effect (for example, natural phenomena such as the wind), direct observation is the first and preferred option. Too often people go straight to the data without even considering direct personal investigation.

For using measurement and metrics with this principle, remember these important provisos:

● **Data is not a substitute for direct observation** Observe first whenever possible.
● **Extrapolated data can lie** Any data used to support observation should come from direct measurement of the activity being studied, not estimated or extrapolated from other information.
● **Do not just measure, analyse** With the experience of direct observation, analyse the processed data and apply critical judgement to understand its meaning.

When making direct observations of the value-creating activity, observers should not be afraid of asking stupid questions. In fact, it can sometimes be quite illuminating for a person with little or no prior knowledge of the process to be part of the observation, as they will come to the task with no preconceptions and may find it easier to keep their focus on what the activity is supposed to actually produce.

2.6.2 Asking questions during observation

Performing observations includes asking questions, particularly the 'why' question. At first, a particular behaviour may seem odd or inappropriate but, once the reason is understood, that perception may change. To be effective, questions should be carefully phrased to take into consideration how the structure of the question may change how it is answered. For example, consider how the answers to these two questions might be different:

● Version 1: Which of the steps in the process is the most annoying to perform?
● Version 2: Which steps in the process, if any, do you think could be simplified?

Both questions might be valid, but the one that should be used will depend on what the questioner is trying to learn. Asking open questions that allow the person answering to formulate their own response can work very well.

It is important to be respectful of the people being observed. This will engender trust and facilitate better understanding of the activities being performed, eliciting greater cooperation from all involved. Observing directly allows a reduction in the use of assumptions, as assumptions if proved unfounded can be disastrous to timelines, budgets and the quality of results.

2.7 BE TRANSPARENT

Bring the work of the service provider out of the darkness and make it as transparent as possible. If more people are aware of what is happening, how it is happening and why it is happening, more people will help and fewer people will obstruct.

When improvement activity occurs in relative silence, or with only a small group being aware of the details, assumptions and rumours can run rampant. Resistance to change will rise, as staff members speculate about what will be changing and how it will impact them. For example, if staff members believe that a move to create efficiency is really intended as an excuse for cutting jobs, obstructionist behaviour will emerge.

2.7.1 Increasing urgency through transparency

When there is poor visibility for improvement activities, there is a risk of creating the impression that the work is of low-priority. When an initiative is communicated to a team, department or company and then is never, or rarely, mentioned again, the perception is that the change is not important. When staff members attempt to prioritize improvement work versus other tasks that have daily **urgency**, improvement work may seem like a low-priority activity unless its importance has been made transparent. Improvement work can be seen as optional, something to attend to only if you can find the time, which is not the case.

2.7.2 Methods for ensuring transparency

The degree of transparency, the level of detail provided, the method used etc. are based on what is useful to the audience in question. For example, when communicating with the business as a whole, the use of existing corporate communications channels to share key high-level accomplishments may be most successful, while inside the IT department, the use of a medium like a Kanban board may be more effective in sharing progress details.

It is important to address the needs of staff members and leaders at all levels. Leaders at various levels should also provide appropriate information relating to the improvement work in their own communications to others. Together, these actions will serve to reinforce what is being done, why it is being undertaken, and how it relates to the stated vision, mission, goals and objectives of the organization. Determining the type, method and frequency of such messaging is one of the central activities related to the critical competency of communication.

Using **CSI register**s to support transparency can be valuable, allowing people to be involved by entering their own improvement suggestions, and leaving registers available and visible to all to keep them apprised of progress towards improvement goals. Encourage managers to communicate to the staff how the content in the CSI registers will be used in the short, medium and long term. In this way staff members see that entering something in a register results in something actually being done.

2.7.3 Keys to success

Another aspect of transparency is ensuring that accomplishments are communicated and celebrated. This will emphasize the importance and value of the effort and instil a sense of pride in those participating. All staff should understand the need to contribute to the improvement activities, which can be reinforced through performance reviews, bonuses and other reward programmes.

2.8 COLLABORATE

When the right people are involved in the right ways, ongoing service provision is more efficient and effective, and improvements benefit from better buy-in, better relevance (because better information is available for decision-making) and better likelihood of long-term success.

Creative solutions, energetic contributions and important perspectives can be obtained from unexpected sources, so inclusion is a better **policy** than exclusion. Cooperation and collaboration are better than the isolated activity frequently referred to as 'silo behaviour'. Recognition of the need for genuine collaboration was one of the driving factors in the evolution of what is now known as DevOps, and without efficient collaboration, neither agile nor Lean techniques will work.

2.8.1 Who to collaborate with

Identifying and managing all types of stakeholders is important. The people and perspectives necessary for successful collaboration can be sourced within the stakeholder groups. In the true sense of the word, a stakeholder is anyone who has a stake in the work of service provisioning, including the providers (internal contributors and external suppliers/partners), the customers and/or the rest of the organization.

A good example is the first and most obvious stakeholder group – the customers. The whole point of being a service provider is to deliver value to them, so they certainly have a stake in ITSM work, but some organizations do a poor job of involving customers. The service provider may feel that it is too difficult to get time from the customer and that the resulting delays are a waste of time. Customers may feel that, after they have defined their requirements, the service provider should just go ahead and deliver the service and, when it comes to process improvement, they may not see any need to be involved at all. In the end, however, the right level of collaboration with the customer throughout the service lifecycle will save time and money and will produce a result that better suits the customer's needs.

2.8.2 Communication for collaboration

For each stakeholder group, their contribution to improvement at each level should be understood and the most effective methods for engaging with them need to be defined. Some contributors may need to be involved at a very detailed level, while others can be involved as reviewers or approvers.

Early in an improvement effort, when goals and objectives are defined, and at critical decision points throughout the process, broad collaboration is critical, particularly in a real-time group context. Everyone needs to be 'in the room' at the same time. While this may be very challenging logistically, it typically saves an enormous amount of work in the long run. Broad support from stakeholders for both the 'what' and the 'how' will also come out of this collaboration, making the initiative much more likely to succeed.

Once the right voices have been heard during key decision-making and clear directions have been agreed, then individuals and teams can work confidently and more independently on their parts of the effort. Building in appropriate collaboration checkpoints and coordination activities ensures continued alignment as the work proceeds.

2.8.3 Scope of collaboration

It should be recognized that the scope of collaboration will vary, based on the scope of impact of the change in question. For example, if an individual team is working on a change to an internal process that has little or no impact on any other team, then minimal collaboration outside the team will be required. It must simply be verified that there are no unaddressed upstream or downstream impacts before proceeding. The organization should decide the amount of autonomy that individuals and teams can have to make their own improvement decisions.

2.8.4 Keys to success

Many methods can be used for effective collaboration, but all require that contributors adopt a respectful attitude towards each other and commit themselves to focusing on what will be best for the company, the customers, suppliers and service provider, not on what would be best for one person or one team. Contributors must feel that they are in an environment in which it is safe for them to express their points of view, and each person must make every attempt to truly understand the points of view of the other contributors so that judgements can be made as objectively as possible.

Having staff members with good facilitation skills is another important success factor, as a good facilitator will be able to set and maintain the appropriate tone and ensure that work does not get bogged down. The group must not endlessly rework the same ground, but must eventually move forward towards actionable conclusions.

When decisions have been made, whether they are about what to do or how to accomplish it, the principle of being transparent should be applied, the decisions should be communicated clearly and appropriately, and the actions to be undertaken explained.

2.9 KEEP IT SIMPLE

If a process, service, action, metric, etc. provides no value or produces no useful outcome, then eliminate it. In a process or procedure, use the minimum number of steps needed to accomplish the objective(s). This may seem obvious, but experience has shown that instances of the principle being applied in the real world are much less common than they should be. The benefits of doing so, however, are many. Overly complex work methods rarely maximize outcomes or minimize cost. When in doubt, look for the simplest, most straightforward method of accomplishing the desired end.

2.9.1 Judging what to keep

When analysing a process, service, metric or other improvement target, always ask the following question: 'Does this create value?' The question is important not only in ITIL, but it is also central to the Lean method. Another way of asking this is to consider, 'Is this fit for purpose and fit for use?' It is better to start simply and carefully add controls, activities or metrics when it is seen that they are truly needed, than to over-complicate or build excessive bureaucracy in the early stages and then try to back off from it later.

Critical to keeping it simple is understanding exactly how something contributes to value. For example, a particular step in a process may be perceived by the staff involved to add no value. To them it may be seen as a waste of time. However, from a corporate perspective, the step may be important to ensuring regulatory compliance and therefore it adds value in an indirect, but nevertheless important, way. Compliance, security, data collection and other concerns may add to the requirements for a process or service and result in more complexity than strictly desirable.

2.9.2 Conflicting objectives

When determining what is truly needed, be mindful of conflicting objectives. For example, management may want to collect a large amount of data for reporting on a process, whereas the people who have to do the record-keeping may want the process to be simpler and not require so much data entry. Through application of the guiding principles (Focus on value; Design for experience; Collaborate; Keep it simple), the group should agree on a balance between the competing objectives. This could mean that only data that will truly provide value will be collected, fields will be automatically populated whenever possible, and the record entry procedures will be simplified to maximize user-friendliness.

2.9.3 Keys to success

We are challenged, in the end, to streamline at every possible point. Creative and collaborative thinking will be required. Challenging old assumptions is necessary. To be successful, be mindful of the human tendency to resist changing old methods, even when the old methods are painful. Just as in managing the customer experience, it is necessary to look at each focus area for improvement in a holistic way, considering in its entirety the flow through people, departments, systems etc. to the desired end. Without a complete view, opportunities for simplification may be overlooked.

2.10 APPLYING THE GUIDING PRINCIPLES

2.10.1 Universal applicability

Time and again organizations have sought ways to improve. Some have tried to do this on their own without the guidance of others, making the same mistakes themselves that hundreds of thousands have made before them. Others try to benefit from the experience of those who have gone before by drawing on the myriad of frameworks, models, methodologies, bodies of knowledge and philosophies that dot the horizon, each one seeming to promise a quick trip to some blissful state in which their current problems have disappeared.

But each new source of assistance often repeats the same recommendations as its predecessors, couching many of the same principles, techniques and guidance in new terminology. But, if giving the same ideas a new twist allows an organization to benefit from them when they would not have done so had the ideas been in their old familiar guise, then so be it.

The principles discussed in this guidance are not specific to ITIL or even to ITSM. They are not useful exclusively in an environment leveraging the guidance in ITIL, nor were they developed uniquely in the writing of ITIL. This is evidenced by the fact that, over and over, we see these underlying principles articulated at the heart of other well-known frameworks, models, methodologies, bodies of knowledge and philosophies. This is not a coincidence. Following these principles works! Many long years of practical experience in organization after organization have proven it. And, conversely, many long years of experience have shown that ignoring these principles frequently leads to failure.

These guiding principles will help service providers to be successful in leveraging the specific practices espoused in any philosophy, framework or methodology, be it ITIL, Lean, DevOps etc.

2.10.2 Multi-framework environments

So what does this mean to an individual working in an organization that is using more than one source of guidance to help with improvements? What if there are proponents of ITIL in the operations team and proponents of agile in the application development group, and proponents of DevOps in the CIO's office? The answer is to focus more on understanding expectations and delivering practical solutions, and less on the purity of any given model or language. Consider:

- Why are we looking for guidance in the first place?
- What are we trying to create or improve?
- What was it about ITIL, agile, DevOps, etc. that made someone think it could be helpful?

When more than one framework is used within an organization, it is not always necessary – or even advisable – to settle on one and eliminate its rivals. For example, a carpenter may have many chisels, each fit for a different task. When used appropriately with a vision of the desired end result, a fine and beautiful piece of furniture can be produced.

In the end, it is not about this framework or that best practice; it is about delivering a better result to the customer. The key is to work together towards the same end. Regardless of the methods or frameworks in use, following them without applying critical thought and adapting the guidance to the specific needs of the organization will not be successful.

These guiding principles should support the organization in achieving its desired goals, using any or all of the available guidance.

3

The CSI approach

This chapter covers:
- Characteristics of the CSI approach
- Step-by-step guide to the CSI approach

3 The CSI approach

The CSI approach is an overarching technique that enables continual service improvement (CSI) for any service provider, and at any organizational level. The CSI approach increases the likelihood of success for IT service management (ITSM) initiatives, puts a strong focus on customer value, and ensures that an individual's work can be more easily linked back to the organization's vision and improvement initiatives. It also allows for timely adjustment of improvement activities by validating success and offering the opportunity to act on what is not working, adjusting plans and approach as needed (see Figure 3.1).

3.1 CHARACTERISTICS OF THE CSI APPROACH

The CSI approach can be applied to improvements at any level of the organization, from strategic, organization-wide initiatives to an individual's day-to-day activities.

It supports an iterative way of working, dividing the work into manageable pieces and reaching the end goal step-by-step, removing the need to look at improvements solely as large – and frequently waterfall-based – initiatives or projects. The CSI approach can be used for any kind of improvement at every stage of the ITIL service lifecycle, with support from strong metrics, effective communication and well-executed organizational change management (OCM), and by applying the guiding principles.

3.1.1 Context for using the CSI approach

Because the CSI approach can be used for any level of improvement, it is important to remember what is motivating the improvement. No one initiates improvement activities when everything is working perfectly. The exact focus of any progression through the steps of the CSI approach will be guided by the goals of the person or group using it and their role within the overall **strategy** of their organization and organizational unit.

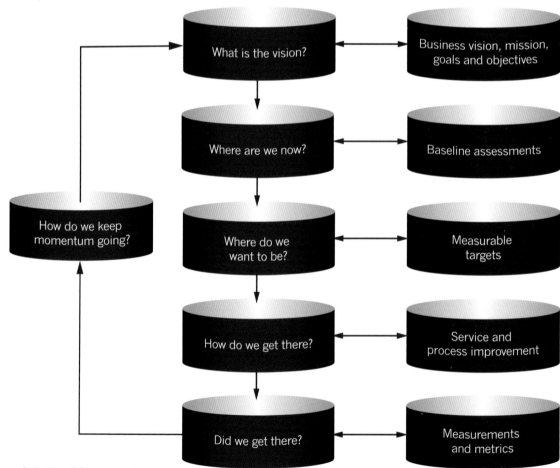

Figure 3.1 The CSI approach

The following sections assume that, whenever the CSI approach is used, it follows a strategy or a high-level objective which suggests the areas for potential improvement. These are usually communicated to a team member by their manager, and linked to higher-level initiatives where specific areas of improvement have been identified. This information could also be found in CSI registers or similar collections of improvement ideas. Sometimes the improvement areas are referred to as technical debt or organizational debt; the list could be an informal collection of ideas, rather than a formal version-controlled document.

High-level objectives for any person or team will be based on their context.

Examples of objectives

Department-level objective for IT

Improve timeliness and cost-effectiveness of key business services in order to enable improved business performance and fund innovation for business processes

This is a broad objective and many individual improvements will be needed to achieve this.

Team-level objective for service desk

Improve customer satisfaction in relation to support calls

This objective is specific to the service desk team, but will still require a set of related improvement initiatives to achieve it.

Individual objective for a service engineer

Improve the availability of high-priority services

This objective is based on the goals of an individual engineer who has a significant role in supporting service availability. The engineer is likely to have some improvements that they can perform themselves, and others that will require significant collaboration across teams, especially with the development and quality assurance specialists.

Note that if this information does not yet exist, or if you are in fact starting a major improvement initiative that would result in the creation of one or more CSI registers, special focus needs to be given to the 'What does the organizational vision mean for me?' part of the orientation worksheet exercise, as described in section 3.2.1.1.

3.1.2 Leveraging the CSI registers

Organizations identify opportunities for improvement in many different ways, at many different times and at many different levels. These opportunities can then be acted upon through the use of the CSI approach. To track and manage improvement ideas from identification through to final action, ITIL recommends the use of a document called a CSI register.

Definition: CSI register

A CSI register is a database or structured document used to record and manage improvement opportunities throughout their lifecycle.

Toolkit

A template for a CSI register can be found in section 7.1.1.

Remember, the template is simply a starting point – your CSI register does not need to look the same or have exactly the same fields.

There can be more than one CSI register in the organization – multiple CSI registers can be maintained on individual, team, department, business unit and organization levels. It does not matter how exactly the information is structured or what the collections of improvement ideas are called in your organization. While the phrase 'CSI register' might be unfamiliar, the concept of capturing improvement ideas most likely is not. Action-item lists are a version of CSI registers. If anyone in the organization is not capturing their improvement ideas in some sort of CSI register, they should be encouraged to start.

Tip

When working with CSI registers, it is important to remember that, because of the complex nature of organizations, every executed improvement can potentially affect other areas of the organization. Therefore a thorough upfront analysis and detailed planning of each and every improvement idea in the CSI register before choosing it for action is not advised, to avoid wasted effort. It is likely that the need for some of the recorded improvement ideas would disappear, as other parts of the organization and/or value network are improved and the circumstances change. Plan wisely.

3.2 STEP-BY-STEP GUIDE TO THE CSI APPROACH

The CSI approach consists of the following six steps:

● **Step 1: What is the vision?**

Each improvement initiative should support the organization's goals and objectives. This step focuses on two key areas.

First, the organization's vision and objectives should be translated for the specific business unit, department, team, and/or individual, so that the context, objectives and boundaries of the improvement initiative are understood. Second, a high-level vision for the planned improvement should be created. The work within this step should ensure that:

- The high-level direction is understood
- The planned improvement initiative is described and understood in the context
- The stakeholders and their role are understood
- The expected value to be realized is understood and agreed
- The role of the person or team responsible for carrying out the improvement is clear in relation to the organization's vision.

If this step is skipped, improvements may only be optimized for the person or team involved, or non-value-added activities may become the sole focus of improvements.

● **Step 2: Where are we now?**

The success of an improvement initiative in an organization depends on a clear and accurate understanding of the starting point and the level of impact the initiative has. This step covers the current state assessment, which may include an assessment of existing services, or elements of the provision of a service, including the customer's perception of value received, people's competencies and skills, **maturity** of processes and procedures, and/or the capabilities of available technological solutions. The organization's culture – the prevailing values and attitudes across all stakeholder groups – should also be understood in order to assess the level of attention OCM requires.

If this step is skipped, the current state will not be understood, and there will not be an objective **baseline** measurement. It will consequently be difficult to track and measure the efficacy of the improvement activities, as it will not be possible to accurately and clearly compare the new state to the previous state when it comes to the subsequent steps of the CSI approach.

- **Step 3: Where do we want to be?**

  Based on the vision for the future and the assessment of the current situation, a **gap analysis** can be performed, improvement opportunities can be identified and prioritized, and improvement objectives can be set. This step ensures the analysis and prioritization of the opportunities has a strong customer focus and is based on the key aspects of services: value, outcome, cost and risk. The agreed objectives, critical success factors (CSFs) and key performance indicators (KPIs) should follow the SMART principle – they should be specific, measurable, achievable, relevant and time-bound. It is much easier to define the travel route when the destination is defined and clearly stated.

  If this step is skipped, the desired future state will remain unclear as 'what good looks like' will not have been defined, and various stakeholders will have a different, if not conflicting, understanding of the end goal. It will also be difficult to prepare a satisfactory answer to the 'What's in it for me?' question for all stakeholders of the improvement initiative, resulting in low support or even significant pushback.

- **Step 4: How do we get there?**

  Based on the understanding of the vision, the current and desired state, and combining that knowledge with subject matter expertise, a plan for addressing the current challenges can be created, communicated and then executed. The plan may be a straightforward direct route to completing a simple improvement, or may involve designing experiments to find the best ways to achieve the desired results. During the improvement, which should follow an iterative approach whenever possible, continual focus should be given to managing risk and measuring progress towards the vision, as well as ensuring visibility and overall awareness of the initiative within the organization. The work of this step takes the initiative to a new current state.

- **Step 5: Did we get there?**

  Too often, once the plan is set in motion, it is assumed that the expected benefits are as good as achieved, and that attention can be redirected to the next initiative. In reality, the path to improvement is filled with various obstacles, and both the progress – 'Have we managed to do what we set out to do?' – and the value – 'Are the previously agreed objectives still relevant?' – of the improvement initiative should be checked and confirmed for each iteration. In this step, progress from the original state towards the agreed desired state should be evaluated, agreed CSFs and KPIs should be checked and the value delivery confirmed. If the desired result has not been achieved, additional actions to complete the work are identified, commonly resulting in a new iteration, after completing the next CSI approach step.

  If this step is skipped, it is difficult to know whether the value was really delivered, and any lessons from this iteration, which would support a course correction if needed, will be lost.

- **Step 6: How do we keep the momentum going?**

  If the improvement initiative delivered the expected value, the focus should now shift to reinforcing new methods and marketing the successes, in order to build support and momentum for additional improvement. True continual improvement is something that is done daily. OCM and knowledge management help to embed the changes in the organization, and ensure the improvements and changed behaviours are not at risk of reverting to their previous state.

  If the expected results were not achieved and the value was not delivered, stakeholders should be informed of the reasons, key lessons should be analysed and learned, and a high-level description of what can be done differently in the next iteration should be provided. The guiding principle of visibility applies both in cases of success and failure, and it is important to remember to avoid blaming individuals, if things did not go as expected – most often, the root cause is elsewhere.

  If this step is skipped, then it is likely the improvements will remain isolated independent initiatives and progress made may be lost again over time. Support for future improvements may also be difficult to obtain and continual improvement will not become a part of the organization's DNA.

The CSI approach should always include all six steps. The scope and scale of effort at each step will vary, however, based on the improvement in question. Keep in mind that the amount of time and effort spent on each step should be appropriate to what is being done and what will be most effective and efficient. It is important to adopt the CSI approach as a mind-set.

The CSI approach may be applied to an entire improvement programme, such as the adoption of ITSM best practices in the organization, as well as at the level of improving an individual service, process or capability. Teams or groups can use the approach to manage their improvement initiatives, and individual contributors can follow the CSI approach to improve their own work area. To reiterate, the CSI approach is not meant solely for large initiatives.

3.2.1 Step 1: What is the vision?

The purpose of this step is to ensure that the organization's vision and its relevance to specific teams and individuals are understood, so that improvement initiatives can be selected, planned, communicated and executed in a way that contributes to achieving the vision. The vision for the specific improvement or improvement area should be described in this step – why is this being looked at, and how does this contribute to the organizational vision? Improvement initiatives can be mapped to the organizational vision using the vision-to-measurement trail (see section 4.3.1), which will help ensure the initiative supports the organization's goals and objectives. In real life, not all the information about the vision and how it relates to specific teams is necessarily available in a ready-to-use format; it may require information mapping to understand the context and constraints.

3.2.1.1 Understanding the context

One of the ways to get a better understanding of the improvement opportunities and challenges is to use the orientation worksheet. The worksheet comprises key questions which can help define an individual's or team's position in the organization and the context, objectives and boundaries for the improvement initiatives. The information on this worksheet can be used by several people, and across multiple improvement initiatives, so it may be advisable to create one worksheet for the whole team, which can be linked to initiative-specific (and individual-specific) elements later on. The worksheet should be revised before each use, to ensure the information it contains is still valid.

Toolkit

A template for an orientation worksheet can be found in section 7.1.2.

What is the organizational vision?

An organization's vision explains the high-level goals the organization wants to achieve. The vision may be expressed as a brief description of a future state, to which all parts of the organization and its value network are required to contribute. The vision focuses on the organization's ambitions, but usually does not detail the ways these will be achieved.

Tip

If you are unsure about the organization's vision, check the organization's website.

Example

San Diego Zoo's official vision statement is:

> *We will lead the fight against extinction.*

(http://zoo.sandiegozoo.org/content/san-diego-zoo-global-mission-and-vision – accessed 26 October 2015).

Albeit brief, a well-written vision statement can confirm the alignment of the proposed idea, plan or course of action with the vision itself. Asking the question 'Does this follow the vision?' can be very useful when assessing improvement ideas.

> ### Example
>
> IT service provider's vision statement:
>
> *We will support our customers in achieving their business objectives by providing reliable and dynamic IT services that support the speed of change required by the ever-changing business environment.*

In the second example, a service provider might want to specify a few more key aspects of the vision, to decrease the ambiguity and help teams to fully align themselves with the vision. This level of abstraction rarely provides a direct answer to the question 'So what should I do, then?' which is why the organization's vision should be translated to team and/or individual level.

What does the organizational vision mean for me?

Every team and every individual in the organization should know how their work contributes to achieving the organization's vision and, by extension, how improving their day-to-day work can help achieve it. This can be expressed through a combination of agreed and documented strategies, objectives, CSFs and KPIs. This information may be communicated to teams and individuals by their manager, and can form part of an IT/ITSM strategy or detailed plan. Organizations have varying abilities to document and communicate vision information. Do not be discouraged if the available information is sparse – it should still provide insight to help you answer the question 'What can I, in my role, do better to support the organization in achieving its vision?' Frequently, the first attempt at answering this question can be made at a team level: 'What can we, as a team, do better to support the organization to achieve its vision?' and an individual's improvement opportunities, aligned with the guiding principles, can then be drawn from the information, based on their role.

As some of this can be described at a rather high level, it could appear that within an individual's role, there is little or no opportunity to impact change and support improvements. It is important not to be discouraged. In Lean, for example, a key principle is that valuable improvement ideas can come from any part of the organization. Frequently, people on the 'factory floor' have the best ideas. However, improvement ideas should be assessed in the context of the organization's vision to ensure they contribute to the overall value flow. The organization is a complex system that performs best not necessarily when each individual component is developed to perfection, but when all components – even if not perfect – work well together. Managers have an important role to play in empowering their teams, and enabling and supporting continual improvement.

>
> ### Tip
>
> Avoid local optimization. It can be quite tempting to begin work on an improvement initiative the moment it has been identified, without clarifying the context. But, by doing so, and skipping the first step in the CSI approach, there is a risk of the improvement becoming simply a local optimization – something that changes an aspect of a service or a service management capability, sometimes only for one group or team – which will not contribute to the delivery of additional value to the customer. In many cases, local optimization can lead to decreased value for the customer, as changing one aspect of the value network can have unexpected negative impact on other parts of the same network.

How am I measured?

The ways in which an individual is measured is a good indication of their work priorities as seen by their manager and the organization. In many organizations, formal personal objectives are agreed annually (or more frequently), and achieving them is usually related to improving the status quo. These improvements should be aligned with the organization's vision and therefore should be supported by the organization as a whole, but the alignment should be confirmed before any significant improvement journey is embarked on. Answering the questions in the orientation worksheet can inform the decisions needed to lower the risk of falling into the local optimization trap.

Where does my work come from and where does it go?

Processes often run across multiple teams and departments, and so does the work. A line manager may be the one who helps to set the overall priorities, but individual requests and tasks can come from different people in different teams, depending on your role and position in the organization. You should understand how their work procedures influence you, and how any potential improvements you are planning might influence them. The same applies to people 'downstream' from you. While many designed interactions are documented in processes and procedures, informal ways of working are often as important, but largely invisible. The complexity of organizational interdependencies can mean that a minor change in one team can lead to huge changes in a team upstream or downstream. Methods such as value stream mapping can be helpful when clarifying the workflows, and both the teams and individuals identified here are likely candidates for stakeholder mapping in the 'What is the vision?' step of the CSI approach (section 3.2.1.2).

Example

As part of an improvement initiative, you might be planning to change the way you prioritize incoming tasks. While this does not conflict with any formal agreements you have with other teams, it might conflict with what has been their experience so far, thus creating confusion. You should ask yourself 'Could this improvement affect them, somehow?' even if the change seems very small. If the answer is 'yes', then this team or individual is a stakeholder for your planned improvement, and needs to be managed.

Who reports to me?

Depending on your role, you might be leading a team of professionals, either with people who report directly to you (as mapped in the organizational chart) or with virtual team members (often the case in matrix organizations, as well as in project teams, with external contractors, etc.). While it might be easier to think that these people have to listen to you, this mind-set is in conflict with the principle of collaboration – these individuals are stakeholders too. When planning improvements, you should not assume that the reporting structure alone is enough to bring people on board. As a manager, you might not be privy to the intricacies of the day-to-day work of your team members, which is why you should seek their input, whenever feasible, to any improvement that could potentially impact them. The same applies to external partners whose contracts you might be managing. The fact that you approve their invoices does not mean they will be on board at once, without being provided with any rationale for the improvements.

While it goes beyond the scope of ITIL to describe and analyse different management theories, the central message in many approaches that support continual improvement is that the manager's role is to support and help to grow, rather than control, their team members. Robert K. Greenleaf's servant leadership principles are one example of such thinking, and this philosophy is widely used in organizations that have embraced agile.

Value stream mapping is also useful for understanding the flow of value through an organization.

3.2.1.2 Mapping the stakeholders

With each step of the CSI approach, it is important to involve and engage stakeholders in the improvement initiative in question, and as such, it is necessary to understand the profiles of each stakeholder and stakeholder group. When correctly filled in, the orientation worksheet will provide a significant amount of information for this exercise.

Identify

Begin identifying the stakeholders by mapping the information to the stakeholder analysis worksheet, which in turn will help to describe the specific characteristics of each stakeholder group for the improvement initiative. The interest column should cover any changes resulting from the improvement, whereas the expectations part should answer the question 'What's in it for me?' from the stakeholder's point of view.

Toolkit

Section 7.4 contains various templates that would be useful for stakeholder management, including a stakeholder analysis worksheet (section 7.4.1).

Analyse

Once the stakeholders have been identified, analyse the processes and workflows relating to the proposed improvement initiative and, using the stakeholder map, divide the stakeholders into four categories: critical, major, significant and minor. This helps to identify the effort required to manage each stakeholder group (for example, communication and status monitoring frequency).

Setting and confirming the goals

It is useful to define the boundaries for the improvement initiative, based on the collected vision information and the area or areas that you believe require attention. All improvement initiatives should have clear goals that clarify both the intent of the improvement, the expected value and the proposed direction – essentially defining the vision for the improvement initiative.

The goals should be concise, future-focused, achievable, clear to all stakeholders and inspiring. As there are many ways that specific goals can be achieved, it is easier to buy into the 'why', compared to the detailed 'how'. Getting into the specifics of an improvement idea without first obtaining buy-in from the stakeholders who will be affected by it leaves the improvement initiative open to resistance.

More information about stakeholder management can be found in section 6.6.2.

3.2.1.3 Outputs from this step

At the conclusion of the 'What is the vision?' step, you should have:

- Information from an orientation worksheet (or other analysis method), including:
  - A clear understanding of the overall organizational vision, mission and goals
  - A clear understanding of the meaning of the vision, mission and goals of your team
  - A clear understanding of your potential contribution to achieving the organizational vision
  - A clear understanding of your position and role in the organization
- An agreed area or areas of focus for a potential improvement initiative to support future investigation, and a described vision of the potential improvement initiative
- A clear understanding of who the stakeholders are, and how they are involved in the improvement initiative in question. This is evidenced by:
  - A completed stakeholder worksheet
  - A completed stakeholder map.

3.2.2 Step 2: Where are we now?

The purpose of the 'Where are we now?' step is to ensure that the current state of the area of focus for the improvement initiative is clearly understood, so that specific improvements can be selected, planned and managed in an effective and efficient manner. The organization's vision provides information about the direction the organization is taking, and confirms whether the day-to-day activities, as well as improvement initiatives, are aligned to the vision. This step, through objective assessment of the current state and through comparison with the expected or desired capabilities and/or performance, will uncover or confirm specific improvement targets that require attention.

3.2.2.1 Assessing and benchmarking

At the heart of the 'Where are we now?' step is the assessment of current capabilities from the point of view of the proposed improvement initiative, which is done to understand the current situation and to create a baseline to compare improvements against. *ITIL V3 Planning to Implement Service Management* (OGC, 2010), section 5.2, lists the following as areas to be measured and assessed:

- Vision and governance
- Steering and strategy
- Processes
- People
- Products, technology and tools
- Culture, service and attitude
- Organizational structure, communication and relationships.

The depth of focus on each of these areas depends on the scope of the assessment. For a large improvement initiative, considerable time can be spent on each area, whereas for a smaller improvement, not all areas need to be covered to that level of detail. That being said, even a seemingly minor improvement may have a wider impact, so it is worth remembering that none of the areas should be completely ignored.

Toolkit

The assessment planning worksheet in section 7.2.6.5 can be used to ensure all relevant areas are covered.

3.2.2.2 Analysing the current state

The data gathered during an assessment is contextualized when the findings around the quality and performance of the previously listed aspects can be benchmarked against a specific model – the industry average, competitor's assessment results, a maturity model, a predefined desired state, or any other relevant source – several of which are listed in the toolkit.

Toolkit

The assessment criteria can be found in section 7.2.5.

More information about **benchmarking** can be found in Chapter 4.

3.2.2.3 A note on process maturity

In the world of ITSM, benchmarking processes and measuring process maturity has sometimes received a disproportionate amount of attention in comparison with other equally relevant aspects, especially around capabilities and organizational culture. In many cases, this has led to inside-out focused initiatives, where the value of the improvement is only seen in process improvements through the service provider's eyes; the customer is expected to benefit from improvements by default.

When assessing process maturity, it is important to remember that, while the maturity models often divide the results into levels, the costs and effort of developing each process to the maximum level (usually '5') is not always justified, which is why a lower maturity level is not necessarily a cause for concern. The most appropriate process maturity level for the organization depends on the business needs – improvement for improvement's sake alone is always a waste. This is not to say higher maturity should not be sought, but it is important to understand whether the organization requires higher levels now or in the future. If the latter is the case, improvement efforts should be targeted at real challenges the organization is facing today.

Having current processes on the highest maturity level is also not necessarily a reason for celebration. It does not automatically lead to value being delivered to customers. If the organization is not yet ready to make use of the higher-level processes due to a shortfall in the overall maturity level, there is a risk of seemingly high maturity processes becoming a source of pain due to a mismatch between needs and capabilities. When the organization is just starting up, formalized processes could become a blocker as the organization is still in discovery mode and the instances of standard work are low, as is the likelihood of being able to understand even the main activities of the organization well enough to design a well-functioning dynamic and flexible process. At the same time, not having formalized processes in place will soon become a blocker for the successful scaling of the business, forcing the organization to focus too much on repetitive work and resolving quality issues, and not allowing enough time to explore new opportunities.

When conducting assessments, make sure all seven of the areas listed in section 3.2.2.1 above are included, and given appropriate focus.

3.2.2.4 Outputs from this step

At the conclusion of the 'Where are we now?' step, you should have:

- A clear understanding of the current state of the improvement area of focus
- Baseline measurements and metrics of the current state to be used for later comparison.

3.2.3 Step 3: Where do we want to be?

The purpose of the 'Where do we want to be?' step of the CSI approach is to reach a common understanding of the desired future state, prioritize the relevant improvements and set detailed targets. It is highly likely that the improvements impact more than one aspect of the current capabilities; i.e. it is not just about people, processes, tools or partners, but rather a combination of these. By the end of this step, we should have a high-level **agreement** on the improvement that is to be undertaken and a readiness to create a detailed action plan.

3.2.3.1 Describing the desired state

The first step of the CSI approach defined or confirmed the overall vision of what the organization would like to achieve, as well as the vision for that part of the organization where you are positioned, and for the improvement area in question. This information, at multiple interconnected levels, creates the context for specific improvements. The second step of the CSI approach established an understanding of the current state in the improvement's focus areas. Do not be overwhelmed by the apparent effort required to achieve the desired state. This situation is not unique to your organization, and the distance between these two states – the future vision and the current reality – is in most cases too great to cross in one go, and requires several (smaller) improvements to reach the destination.

In this step you need to define what you want to achieve with a specific improvement, ensuring that the improvement objectives:

- are aligned with the overall vision, to ensure that the right direction is kept
- have agreed measurable targets, to ensure that success can be verified
- have been prioritized appropriately, to ensure that effort is not wasted on insignificant areas and that dependencies are managed well
- are supported by stakeholders, to ensure continual support for the initiative.

Regardless of whether or not the desired state is mapped out clearly, or whether there are still many adjustments to be made, it is important to know 'what good looks like'. It is equally important to communicate the desired state to all stakeholders in a language they understand, focusing on benefits relevant to them. Remember that the improvement is most likely a part of a larger improvement which contributes to somebody else's desired state upstream, which is why it is vital that the definition of the desired state the improvement should deliver aligns with the organization's vision. Once a definition that satisfies these criteria has been successfully created, convincing the stakeholders of the value of the improvement will be much easier.

Often, as the desired state is being defined, the nature of the stakeholders' needs and requirements will become more apparent. This information might be available in various knowledge management systems and document repositories, but that is not always the case. Work directly with the stakeholders to make further discoveries, ensure all assumptions have been documented, and make certain that the findings have been correctly understood. A good way to carry out these discovery sessions is to run stakeholder workshops.

Toolkit
The workshop and meeting action plan can be found in section 7.3.2.

Once the expectations are understood, use a structured model – for example, the one used in section 3.2.2 to **benchmark** the current status – for a holistic approach when describing the desired state. Remember to focus on capabilities, rather than processes. This will help to avoid falling into the trap of an internally focused (technical) desired state description. The improvement should not focus purely on, for example, getting demand management processes from Level 2 to Level 4. Rather, the focus should be on supporting the customer better with the help of an improved process as part of the overall capability. This part of the improvement should be balanced with the other three Ps of the People-Process-Products-Partners matrix, keeping the focus on quality and customer satisfaction.

Chapter 4 describes various organizational cascades that help to connect the desired future state to a larger vision, while ensuring all relevant aspects of the improvement initiative have been covered.

3.2.3.2 Performing a gap analysis

A gap analysis allows a comparison between the desired future state and the current state to be made, identifying the potential individual improvements by comparing the benchmarking data with the desired state description:

- Are the current goals and strategy aligned with the organization's vision?
- Are the values and attitudes aligned with the organization's vision?
- Are the required skills and competencies available?
- Are the required supporting processes and procedures available?
- Is the required supporting technology available?

Toolkit
An example of a gap analysis can be found in section 7.2.6.4.

3.2.3.3 Categorizing and prioritizing improvements

The results of the gap analysis have most likely populated the CSI registers with a number of individual improvement ideas. These ideas should be prioritized based on the expected value for the customer and alignment with the organization's vision. At this stage, the improvement ideas will not be very detailed. Areas for improvement may be identified, but the specific actions are usually not. This is the focus of the next step in the CSI approach. Each of the improvement ideas in this step could be seen as a challenge – or obstacle,

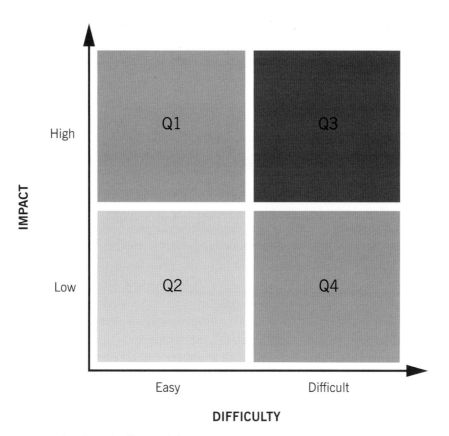

Figure 3.2 Improvement categorization matrix

as these are sometimes called – to overcome to reach the desired future state. Not all potential areas are equal in terms of impact and value. It is helpful to utilize an objective method, such as an improvement categorization matrix, as seen in Figure 3.2, to understand the priorities.

Quadrant 1 improvements are the **quick wins**, where the positive impact of the improvement is the highest, while the effort required to execute the improvement is the lowest. These improvements are the most likely candidates for immediate execution.

Quadrant 2 improvements, although having a low impact, are excellent candidates to show immediate progress and ensure continual buy-in from the stakeholders.

Quadrant 3 improvements are valuable, but require more time and effort to execute. Often these are the strategic initiatives that involve more stakeholders. You should confirm whether it is possible to further split these improvements into smaller, less complicated improvements.

Quadrant 4 improvements require the highest effort while delivering the lowest impact. While useful to document and analyse, these improvements are less likely to be selected for execution.

Although most of the individual improvement ideas can be placed in one of the four quadrants of the matrix, which will help with prioritization, there might also be emergency improvements which are not optional and cannot be delayed, regardless of the effort required.

Impact and dependencies

As long as the improvement is aligned with the vision and the expected value to be delivered is clear, the largest improvement does not necessarily need to be the one that gets implemented first. Even small improvements – and often, especially these – will be of great help to the organization. *ITIL Service Design*, section 8.1, provides additional context for **business impact analysis (BIA)**.

Definition: Business impact analysis

Business impact analysis is the activity in business continuity management that identifies vital business functions and their dependencies. These dependencies may include suppliers, people, other business processes, IT services etc. Business impact analysis defines the recovery requirements for IT services. These requirements include recovery time objectives, recovery point objectives and minimum service level targets for each IT service.

Finally, when planning improvements it is important to consider if any of the improvements to be undertaken have any dependencies between them. Perhaps one improvement will be unsuccessful unless another improvement is completed first. Perhaps the timing of the implementation of several improvements will be important to ensuring overall success. Dependencies should be addressed wherever possible to avoid conflict and/or failure of improvement efforts. This aspect of prioritization will influence which improvements are selected for action, and will also be an important part of the 'How do we get there?' step of the CSI approach.

3.2.3.4 Setting and agreeing the targets

At this point, specific improvements from the CSI registers are selected to be undertaken, based on the gap analysis and how the individual improvement ideas fit into the larger improvement or change initiatives. In most cases, continuing with a few selected improvements is preferable to trying to address all potential improvements at once. Added to which, it might not be wise to implement several improvements in parallel that each addresses the same challenge, as this is likely to lead to duplicated effort, could potentially have an opposite effect due to various changes cancelling each other out, and would make it harder to learn which course of action was most efficient.

The 'Where are we now?' step should have provided the 'before' picture for each proposed improvement. Now we need to create the desired 'after' picture with more detailed, preferably SMART objectives, CSFs and KPIs. When larger improvement initiatives are broken down into smaller ones, each of these has its own CSFs and KPIs defined, and each of these supports the higher-level objectives. Section 4.2 discusses SMART in greater detail.

Toolkit

The CSF worksheet in section 7.2.1 will help to identify and describe individual CSFs.

An individual KPI worksheet can be used to define individual KPIs for each CSF, and can be found in section 7.2.2.

To verify that the KPIs for each area are well balanced, use the KPI balance checklist in section 7.2.3.

3.2.3.5 Evaluating the viability

As the targets for the proposed improvements are clarified, more information should be available to help evaluate whether the proposed improvement(s) are viable. Ensure:

● The improvement fits with the priorities, and is achievable considering any constraints there might be

● The relevant stakeholders can be convinced and influenced to successfully carry out this improvement.

Even when an initiative is aligned to the organization's vision, the team who initiated it might not be in the best position to deliver the expected value. Collaboration across the organization is the key here, and it might be more efficient to support another team – with more resources and/or stronger backing – to deliver this improvement instead.

At other times, the organization as a whole is not ready to support the initiative. Recognizing that this is the case before the initiative starts can save time and may avoid unnecessary frustration when well-meant and seemingly well-planned improvements fail for no apparent reason. In these cases, more often than not the stakeholder needs have not been understood. Sometimes, the planned outcomes of a given initiative are in direct conflict with the stakeholders' true objectives.

While the key stakeholders have already been identified, now that the focus is on specific improvement initiatives, it is possible to take a closer look. While assessing the situation on this level of detail, new relevant information might emerge about, for example, the stakeholders or the constraints regarding the execution of the improvements. Answering the following questions will help assess the viability of the initiative in question.

Who can be influenced?

It is important to understand the informal structure of the part of the organization that is impacted by the improvement. Subtle nuances can have a major impact on the viability of the improvement initiative. Each of the people in the sphere of influence should be mapped – many of whom might not be part of the reporting line. As with all stakeholders, answering the question 'What's in it for me?' from their point of view makes it much easier to explain the rationale behind the proposed improvement.

Who needs to be convinced?

Individuals in the organization whose buy-in for the improvement needs to be secured should be identified. In many cases, this might be the line manager, but for improvements of significant complexity, the circle of people who need to be convinced widens. This group of people also includes potential sponsors for the initiative.

The higher the levels of resistance to change in the organization, the more support is required for successful improvement initiatives. More information about managing sponsors can be found in Chapter 6, and the stakeholder and sponsorship tools described in the toolkit (Chapter 7) help map the sponsors and their relationships in the organization.

Toolkit

The sponsor diagram can be found in section 7.4.4 (Figure 7.5).

The sponsor roadmap is in section 7.4.5.

Are there other related initiatives?

It is important to become familiar with other ongoing improvement initiatives within the organization in order to ensure the work being undertaken does not conflict with other initiatives, or does not become irrelevant because another initiative has already resolved a specific challenge. Many of these could be revealed in conversations with stakeholders, though sometimes the information needs to be sought out. If improvement activities are tied in with business-as-usual (BAU) work, these might not be apparent and possibly will not be mentioned when discussing ongoing initiatives. Other teams' CSI registers can also be a good source of information – though be aware that similar initiatives might go by a variety of names. Talk to the CSI manager, if there is one, as this person typically has visibility into many if not all the other efforts underway. They could quickly point in the right direction.

What are the constraints?

When assessing the viability of any improvement initiative, it is crucial to understand the constraints. Some are fixed, which means they are inescapable, while others are situational, and can possibly be influenced. For any improvement that requires an investment, ensure that the budget is available and that the cost will be approved by the relevant stakeholders. There might also be other constraints that are related to time, skills, technology etc.

In complex environments, a seemingly disproportionate stakeholder management effort can be required to support an improvement initiative. Rather than fighting the reality, this should be acknowledged and approached appropriately. It is important to remember that achieving success with an improvement initiative is unlikely unless all stakeholders have been identified and are being managed at an appropriate level. A great idea on its own will not suffice: to succeed, others need to be convinced of its value.

To better understand what can be achieved, map the driving (positive) and restraining (negative) influencing factors using the force field analysis, described in the toolkit. As different forces have different strengths, it is important to rate each and then analyse the results. If the analysis shows strong restraining forces, address those specifically and convert them to driving forces, where possible. As long as the improvement initiative is successfully mapped to the organizational vision and the stakeholders have been properly analysed, other teams and individuals can be of great help in selling the improvement idea, as well as in helping to execute the improvement. A genius idea can be left with no support if the connection with the organization's vision (and therefore, with other teams' goals and objectives) is not clear.

Toolkit

Force field analysis is featured in section 7.4.11.

3.2.3.6 Creating and presenting a business case

Definition: Business case

A business case is a justification for a significant item of expenditure. The business case includes information about costs, benefits, options, issues, risks and possible problems.

Every improvement initiative, regardless of its size, requires agreement and support from stakeholders, based on a justification that makes sense to them. A **business case** is the tool that is used to communicate what we propose to do and why, so that stakeholders can use it for decision support and can feel confident that the right path is being followed.

There is no one true format for a business case; as long as it serves its purpose, any format is acceptable. Different proposed improvements may require dramatically different levels of information in order to gain the support of stakeholders and reach an agreement on the desired end state. While large initiatives could indeed require a thorough and lengthy business case, for smaller initiatives, one paragraph of text sent in an email might be sufficient.

As with any other customer-focused artefact, when creating a business case for the improvement, it is important to describe it from the reviewer's/approver's point of view, as it is meant to be understood and used by them. The creation of a business case can be a valuable exercise in more ways than one, as the process of creating it may require you to sharpen the focus and the targets of the improvement and validate their alignment with the overall vision.

All known assumptions should be documented as part of the business case, and the larger the proposed improvement initiative, the more attention should be given to understanding and documenting the assumptions. Failing to do so may lead to a myriad of surprises during the execution of the improvement, and is likely to make stakeholders lose confidence.

Toolkit

Business cases are discussed in section 7.3.4.

3.2.3.7 Reaching agreement

By the end of this step, an agreement on the improvements that will be undertaken should be in place and, if there is more than one, the priority for implementation as well. This was hopefully achieved after the stakeholders reviewed the business case and granted their approval. However, it may be that, upon evaluating the business case, stakeholders still have questions or concerns. In that case, it may be necessary to do more research or to provide more details of how the objectives will be achieved, essentially providing some of the 'How do we get there?' details, or going back and redefining the objectives and metrics for the initiative.

Striking the right balance between a business case that is too high-level to obtain informed approval from stakeholders, and spending too much effort on designing the specifics before getting a 'yes' to proceed, is a delicate matter. Determine the course that is most likely to succeed based on experience and the specific circumstances, and then revise the approach as needed. Over-complication is likely to lead to many (undocumented) assumptions being included, and the intent behind the initiative can get lost in the detail.

3.2.3.8 Outputs from this step

At the conclusion of the 'Where do we want to be?' step, you should have:

● A description of the desired future state
● The results of a gap analysis, demonstrating current deficiencies
● A prioritized list of improvements with associated SMART objectives and balanced KPIs, where possible
● A clear understanding of the constraints that may influence what you can improve
● A business case for the improvement initiative
● Agreement from stakeholders to go forward with the proposed improvements and any associated priorities.

3.2.4 Step 4: How do we get there?

The purpose of the 'How do we get there?' step of the CSI approach is to define an execution plan for the selected improvements based on the outputs of the previous steps, and to carry out the improvements. If the planning activities in this step reveal significant new information that might impact stakeholders' expectations or support for the improvement, go back to the previous steps of the CSI approach, re-engage with the stakeholders, and seek their confirmation before the action plan can be agreed and improvements executed.

3.2.4.1 Context for planning

Depending on the size of the improvement, there may be established methods or requirements in your organization that govern how planning and delivery of improvements are conducted. Find out what is already in place in your organization to ensure established policies are complied with, as well as whether any existing artefacts, such as tools and templates, can be leveraged.

3.2.4.2 Creating the plan

Each improvement initiative requires planning regarding how it will be delivered. Managing an initiative does not mean starting with an overcrowded Gantt chart, or even that a Gantt chart is needed. Continuous delivery of small improvements is often preferred to long waiting periods and big-bang changes, but depending on the nature of the improvement, this might not always be possible. It helps to complete as much of the due diligence work as possible as part of a higher-level improvement initiative, so that smaller initiatives do not require a lengthy sign-off procedure, and can be executed rapidly within a context of understood and accepted risks and impact.

Planning and control methods

Structured project management methods (e.g. PRINCE2 Agile) can help with visibility and governance at all stakeholder levels, and should be combined with specific flow management and delivery methodologies and techniques – for example, Scrum or Kanban – for best results. Some levels of management might not be obviously visible, which might create the impression that certain planning and reporting activities are an unnecessary overhead. While the team's work could be managed in, for example, two-week sprints using Scrum, or could be predominantly categorized as BAU, the deliverables are likely to feed into a larger initiative – product development, capability improvement, upstream BAU etc. – which in turn feeds into an even larger initiative, and so forth, all targeted at achieving the organization's vision, as outlined in the strategy. Each of these levels has its own requirements for planning and reporting, to ensure visibility and continual support.

The nature of the initiative should be understood, as well as the individual's role in it, to choose the best planning and delivery approach. It is also necessary to understand how the initiative relates to other initiatives that might be running in parallel, on more strategic or tactical levels. The completion of the orientation worksheet during the 'What is the vision?' step (section 3.2.1) should have assisted in ensuring that this understanding of context, interconnectivity and dependence has been maintained throughout.

Figure 3.3 illustrates different levels of governance and delivery, where initiatives are being planned and executed using various methodologies.

Regardless of the chosen delivery method, the plan should be designed to be as efficient and lightweight as possible while ensuring the stakeholders have the required levels of visibility and control, and that any regulatory requirements are taken into account and followed. An overly complicated approach that cannot be justified by regulations and/or does not deliver additional value ends up hindering work, and is not an example of successfully applying best practice.

Planning iterations

While dividing improvements into manageable iterations that deliver value frequently is often the best approach, the organization might not have experience with this way of working. Time is likely to be needed for people to adjust to more agile and iterative ways of working. The concept of quick wins is widely understood, and delivering value through quick wins can be a successful approach to introducing agile methods into your organization.

The delivery approach and plan for the improvement should be designed by working with the stakeholders, rather than in isolation, which would reduce the potential for unpleasant surprises later on. Constraints should be analysed and assumptions should be documented. Risk analysis should also be performed. Be aware that people naturally prefer certainty over uncertainty, and sometimes an illusion of certainty is taken as real, or

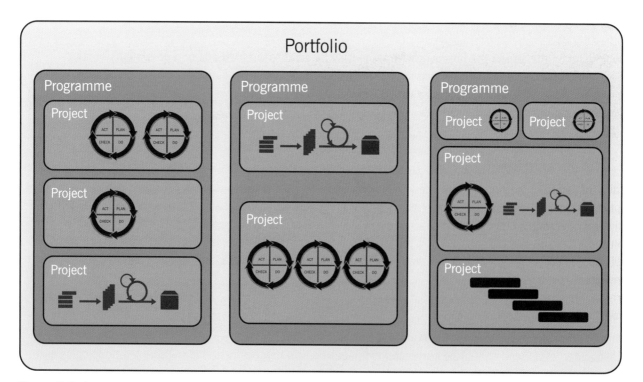

Figure 3.3 An example of initiatives planned and executed

certainty is demanded where there can be none. It is imperative to remember that, in many cases, creating an accurate long-term (6+ months) detailed plan is not possible due to uncontrollable circumstances and lack of information. Presenting such a plan could do a disservice to the initiative and its stakeholders by creating a false sense of certainty and confidence, and leaving them unprepared for adjusting the plan going forward. Instead, describing the short-term activities in more detail, while keeping the long-term activities at a higher level, means that lessons learned can be taken into account within the plan while progressing further with the initiative. If a detailed long-term plan is still required to initiate the improvement, carefully document all assumptions used when creating the plan. Over time, the successful application of the iterative small-step approach – delivering value quickly and consistently and allowing often-unprecedented flexibility when a change of course is needed – should help with generating confidence in stakeholders, even with only short-term detailed plans.

It is highly probable that a lot of the required information will be unknown at the start of the improvement. For this reason, it is acceptable (and often, advisable) to use the early iterations to gather more information, which can be used to improve the overall plan. A successful outcome of those iterations is not an implemented improvement as such, but an improved understanding of the situation, challenges and potential solutions, as well as the customer's feedback on this.

3.2.4.3 Communicating the plan

Each improvement initiative needs to define the roles and responsibilities for all stakeholders and actors involved. One of the most simple and most widely used techniques to map the roles is use of a **RACI** matrix – dividing stakeholders into groups of being responsible, accountable, consulted and informed. Section 6.2 covers the RACI matrix in more detail.

Toolkit

The RACI model authority matrix can be found in section 7.4.6.

Once the plan has been designed, it can be presented to the stakeholders. Communicating the plan helps to set expectations. Once the plan has been signed off, the work on the improvement can begin. A stakeholder communication plan can help you to design and track the communication activities required to successfully prepare and deliver the presentation.

Toolkit

A communication success criteria worksheet can be found in section 7.3.5. A stakeholder communication plan template can be found in section 7.4.3.

3.2.4.4 Implementing the plan

While the name of this step of the CSI approach is 'How do we get there?' which might imply it finishes with a plan, the step also includes engaging in the work defined in the plan. As always, iteration and timely adjustment as circumstances change are critical to success. The metrics defined to evaluate success should be used to validate progress as the work goes on. Also, it is important to remember that there may be several individual improvement iterations occurring in parallel. One may be close to completion and have moved on to the 'Did we get there?' step, while others are still early in the 'How do we get there?' step and others are further along in the same step. The plan should take this into consideration and the governance methods should accommodate efficient management of improvement activities of many types.

3.2.4.5 Testing potential solutions

The approach taken to plan and deliver the improvements depends on the nature of the challenge at hand. With some improvements, the solution is abundantly clear and the plan can be relatively straightforward – an agreed approach that has been used previously for similar improvements might exist, or there could be a predefined procedure for improvements in a specific area.

However, it is quite possible that while the objective to be achieved is clear, the exact solution to achieve that objective is not. Which potential path will lead to achieving the agreed objective? For example, consider the following improvement:

> Reduce the number of emergency capacity changes to production servers by 50% within four months.

This objective is specific. It can be measured. It was scoped based on what was believed to be achievable and was judged to be relevant to overall goals, and it is time-bound. But what specific improvement actions will cause this objective to be achieved? Is it clear why there are so many emergency capacity changes? Is there agreement on the most likely practices, technology, training etc. to reduce the number of emergency capacity changes in the amount and timeframe required?

In situations like this, potential solutions should be defined and tested to determine the correct course of action. Essentially, we are using structured experimentation to make the desired improvement as efficient as possible, while addressing the uncertainty. The improvement plan should be designed to include this work in a structured way, without working haphazardly or based on instinct alone.

When to use experimentation

When is experimentation appropriate? Thinking in terms of the predictability of outcomes can be useful here. After all, no one wants to waste time on an effort that is unlikely to produce the required results. When assessing the challenge to be addressed by the improvement, the questions listed in Table 3.1 are useful.

Table 3.1 When to use experimentation

Question to ask	What to do if the answer is 'yes'
Do you know, without extensive further analysis, which action(s) to perform to get the expected result?	While care needs to be taken to make sure the situation has not been oversimplified, in most cases existing solutions and models can be used to run the improvement.
Do you require additional analysis to choose between potential actions to get the expected result?	Apply your domain-specific knowledge, assess various options and decide on a course of action. To avoid jumping to conclusions and the effects of unconscious biases, you should discuss the proposed actions with your peers before confirming the approach.
Do you have ideas on what could be an effective action, but lack specific previous experience and concrete evidence, or does the evidence support multiple, often contradictory, solutions?	You should define a well-formulated hypothesis, design and execute an experiment or a series of experiments (in parallel or sequentially).

The scientific method

For those who wish to further formalize their approach to experimentation, guidance may be found in the scientific method. The material here introduces some of the key concepts of the scientific method, but to leverage this method successfully, a deeper study would be advisable.

Definition: Scientific method

Principles and procedures for the systematic pursuit of knowledge involving the recognition and formulation of a problem, the collection of data through observation and experiment, and the formulation and testing of hypotheses (Merriam-Webster).

The scientific method allows hypotheses to be tested in a controlled manner in order to learn and find the best solution to the challenge at hand. This method is not specific to ITSM, or even to IT. The same approach is shared in all sciences, and it is an efficient way to acquire solid new knowledge in an unfamiliar domain. Table 3.2 contains an example of how the scientific method could be divided into specific actions.

Table 3.2 An approach to the scientific method

1	Analyse the situation	Observe the area of challenge
2	Formulate a question	What do you want to know?
3	Research the field	Familiarize yourself with the domain
4	Formulate a hypothesis	What do you think the answer could be?
5	Design the experiment	What would verify or falsify the hypothesis?
6	Test the hypothesis	Run the experiment
7	Analyse the results	Confirm data accuracy
8	Make a conclusion	Decide whether the hypothesis was verified/falsified
9	Attempt to replicate	Ensure the results were not a random glitch

The hypothesis is an important concept within the scientific method. The scientific method places extra rigour around the use of the hypothesis. Both the expected outcomes and the conditions for the experiment should be formulated in order to ensure the hypothesis is both testable and falsifiable.

Definition: Scientific hypothesis

An idea that proposes a tentative explanation about a phenomenon or a narrow set of phenomena observed in the natural world. The two primary features of a scientific hypothesis are falsifiability and testability, which are reflected in an 'If...then' statement summarizing the idea and in the ability to be supported or refuted through observation and experimentation.

(http://www.britannica.com/topic/scientific-hypothesis – accessed 26 October 2015)

Hints for using experimentation in ITSM

In the context of ITSM improvements, it makes sense to design experiments so that they support quick feedback from customers, and it is important not to be discouraged by falsified hypotheses as you progress – both verified and falsified hypotheses are successful. In case of falsification, it is better to fail fast, learn fast, regroup and design the next experiment, rather than spend considerable time working on something, only to find it does not work later on after significant investment.

Evaluate whether it is possible to run several experiments in parallel in order to cover more ground and get a more complete picture of what the best approach is. If this is possible, try to design mutually exclusive experiments, where the positive outcome of one experiment must mean a failure of at least one other.

3.2.4.6 Outputs from this step

At the conclusion of the 'How do we get there?' step, you should have:

- An approved action plan, aligned with stakeholders' requirements for governance
- An understanding of the nature of the improvements and the most efficient method to be used to reach the expected results
- Completed improvement actions, based on the previously communicated and approved plans.

3.2.5 Step 5: Did we get there?

The purpose of the 'Did we get there?' step of the CSI approach is to confirm whether the desired future state has been reached, going beyond anecdotal evidence to utilize data analysis to confirm the new status, as well as confirming the value delivered with the stakeholders.

3.2.5.1 Confirming the value delivery

In the 'Where do we want to be?' step, the relevant CSFs and KPIs for the improvement were confirmed. Various assessment techniques, for example the techniques used in the 'Where are we now?' step, can be brought in to assess the new state.

Checking the CSFs and KPIs

Many of the measuring activities can be done during the improvement initiative, using metrics, surveys etc., and preferably utilizing automation. With a longer improvement, which might take several months before the desired future state has been achieved, it is inadvisable to wait until the end of the initiative to confirm the correctness of the approach. If the data does not support the decisions made, the approach should be reviewed and, if necessary, tweaked, or alternatively, a new iteration should be started, using lessons learned as input.

Carrying out a benefits realization review

Although monitoring the KPIs can provide instant insight into the success of the improvement initiative while it is still running, confirming the CSFs might not be possible before the initiative has been completed.

The benefits realization review should be carried out after the completion of the 'How do we get there' step for each improvement, and this should be done for all improvements, not just major improvement initiatives. While the effort that goes into completing the review depends on the scope, the concept of confirming the realization of the expected benefits is crucial to ensuring the continuity of the improvement initiatives.

Be cautious not to fall into the 'watermelon' service level agreement (SLA) type of assessment, where everything looks OK (green) on the outside, but inside it is all broken (red). Comparing the metrics data is not the only aspect that needs to be checked; the stakeholders need to confirm the value was actually delivered.

The benefits review should use the following artefacts as the basis for the assessment:

- Business case for stakeholders and high-level benefits
- Agreed CSFs for detailed benefits
- Execution plan for timelines and responsibilities.

When presenting the results to the stakeholders, make use of the report worksheet to ensure the information presented is in the right format and the required actions from the report are clear.

Toolkit

The benefits realization review template can be found in section 7.1.3.

Toolkit

The report worksheet can be found in section 7.2.4.

3.2.5.2 Outputs from this step

At the conclusion of the 'Did we get there?' step, you should have:

● Completed and verified results from previously defined improvement initiatives and objectives

● A completed benefits review document.

3.2.6 Step 6: How do we keep the momentum going?

3.2.6.1 Ensuring continuity

The following key principles can help to improve the chance of success of the improvement initiatives and ensure its continuity:

● Understanding the organization's vision

● Understanding the gap between the current state and the desired future state

● Correct prioritization, based on the value for the customer

● Correct identification and management of stakeholders

● Correct level of detail in the business case, presented from the stakeholders' point of view

● Correctly identified risks and thought-through mitigation plans

● Correctly structured delivery plan, supporting regulatory and governance requirements

● Continual visibility of the progress and the status of the initiative for all stakeholders

● A completed benefits review as a part of each improvement iteration.

The closed-loop nature of the feedback in the CSI approach allows for lessons learned to be fed back to higher-level improvement initiatives, making sure efficient ways of working prevail and inefficient ways are abandoned.

3.2.6.2 Institutionalizing improvements

At this point in the CSI approach, individual improvements that were planned have been completed, and the results achieved have been verified. That does not, however, guarantee that the benefits achieved will not erode over time, or that new behaviours that have been instituted will not be abandoned. In order to keep the forward momentum, it will frequently be necessary to take actions to embed the changes more firmly in the organization. Examples of actions that may be taken include:

● Follow-on training, both formal and informal, to further solidify understanding of the new ways

● Regular review of reports and metrics to validate that benefits achieved are not eroding

● Conducting roundtable sessions with stakeholders of various types after changes have been in place for a while to gather feedback from them on how well the changes are working. Waiting for some time to pass will allow the stakeholders to develop a deeper, more informed and practical view of the value of the change.

OCM can offer excellent guidance on creative ways of embedding or 'institutionalizing' the change so that the hard work of improvement provides the maximum value it can.

3.2.6.3 Supporting a learning organization

The nature of the focus of improvements can vary significantly, depending on the organization. Where service management capabilities are less mature, the early rounds of improvements may have a strong inward focus (e.g. process improvements), which can indirectly benefit the customer. More mature organizations may find it easier to define improvements with a more explicit outward focus (e.g. service improvement). This progression is normal and the difference of focus is not something that should be avoided. Depending on the organization's current ability to deliver clearly defined value, it may make sense to concentrate on service provider-focused improvements first. The quick wins achieved during these improvements – as long as they are aligned with the organization's vision – are likely to buy goodwill from the customer, and prepare them for more partnership-focused discussions. There is no need to draw disproportionate attention to the improvements – while visibility should be there for stakeholders, they are not often interested in details about technical/inward-focused improvements.

Leading by example

Extra effort may be required, in addition to agreed daily activities, to prepare the organization for the continual improvement philosophy. Often, setting an example is an efficient way to gain support. The whole organization does not necessarily need to buy into the continual improvement at once. After some time, when they have seen the team practising the new methods and techniques and delivering additional value for the customer and the organization, it is highly likely that other teams will be interested in learning the secrets of success.

Integrating CSI into normal work practices

In the long run, the aim should be to make continual improvement a part of normal work, not something that is an extra-curricular activity. Continually monitoring progress in preparation for changes of course, as well as a strong commitment to OCM, is crucial. Most often, improvements do not fail because the idea behind the improvement was not good enough, but because the human factor was severely underestimated. People involved in the initiatives need to be empowered to make decisions and take action. When progress diverts from the plan, people should not be discouraged from taking the next steps, but lessons should always be learned. When it comes to formal reviews of the improvement outcomes, remember – the root cause for any failure is rarely an individual. Treat challenges as chances for further improvement.

Every organization is a complex adaptive system – all elements of this system interact and influence each other's behaviour, which is why it is impossible to accurately predict or control all of the results of change introduced in the organization. It is difficult, if not impossible, to directly change the culture in the organization, but it is possible to influence the organization's behaviour (Ashkenas, 2011; Katzenbach et al., 2012).

In addition to the guidance in this chapter, there are various other methods and techniques available, focusing on the same core concept of continual iterative improvement, aimed at increasing value for the customers. One of the most notable of these and widely used in the Lean community is the Improvement Kata, based on Toyota's approach to continual improvement (Rother, 2009). More details about contextualizing challenges and finding the most appropriate responses can be found in frameworks such as Cynefin (Snowden and Boone, 2007).

3.2.6.4 Outputs from this step

At the conclusion of the 'How do we keep the momentum going?' step, you should have:

● Firmly established changes from the executed improvements
● An understanding of how to support continual improvement in the organization going forward.

4

Metrics and measurement

This chapter covers:

- What is measurement for?
- Critical success factors and key performance indicators
- Metric cascades and hierarchies
- Metric categories
- Assessments
- Reporting
- Continual improvement of metrics and measurement

4 Metrics and measurement

Metrics and measurement lie at the core of IT service management (ITSM) and of continual service improvement (CSI). It is important to measure what is being done and what is being delivered, in order to understand what is working well and what needs to be improved, to demonstrate value to the business and customers, and to enable more objective decisions to be made. Then you should act on what is discovered.

Definitions of the terms 'metric' and 'measurement' can be found in section 4.3.1, but for now it is enough to know that a measurement is an individual piece of data that can be collected, and a metric is something calculated from one or more measurements.

Some things are easy to measure and some may be more difficult, but everything can be measured if it is sufficiently important. The book *How to Measure Anything* (Hubbard, 2014) describes a measurement as a 'reduction of uncertainty based on one or more observations'. If it is necessary to know how satisfied a customer is, or what a particular service costs, or how reliable a technology component is, then identify the observations that can be made to provide the information needed. These could be: simple observations with a low level of accuracy; more sophisticated measurements using freely available tools; or the design of a complex measurement framework and the procurement of more expensive tools to make comprehensive measurements. Decisions about how accurate the measurement needs to be, and how much time, money and effort are available to get that level of accuracy, are important aspects of metrics and measurement.

Many IT service providers seem to believe that anything that can be measured should be measured. They may define hundreds of key performance indicators (KPIs) and generate long reports showing how IT has performed against each of them. Those who are familiar with the ITIL guidance will know that it contains many examples of KPIs. Adopting all of the KPIs in the core ITIL publications would provide 355 things to measure and report. Of course, the KPIs in ITIL are examples, and nobody is expected to adopt all 355 of them. It is important to be selective.

Adopting too many KPIs can make it hard to identify the ones that really matter. A report that shows 250 targets that were met and 105 that were missed does not help to identify and prioritize what needs to be improved. The sheer volume of data tends to drown out the significant information. A very small number of well thought-out KPIs will generally prove far more valuable. It is acceptable to collect data that is not actually used in reports, because this data might be useful in specific circumstances but not others. Try to avoid collecting data that definitely will not be used, and definitely avoid creating reports that include unnecessary data.

Tip

Measuring and reporting a small number of well-focused KPIs can help with managing IT services. Adding more KPIs can deliver less value, because you lose focus on what is important. Keep the number of KPIs you measure and report as small as possible.

The metrics and measurements that are defined will influence the behaviour of staff members and customers, and the culture of the organization. It is important to consider every metric in terms of how it will influence behaviour, as well as how well it measures the things that are considered important.

This chapter will help to identify why measurements need to be made, what should be measured, what does not really need to be measured, and how to use measurements to best effect.

4.1 WHAT IS MEASUREMENT FOR?

Before starting an activity, always ensure the goals and objectives are understood. This is just as true for defining what needs to be measured as it is for creating a new IT service or improving a process. So, what are the goals and objectives of measurement?

As shown in Figure 4.1, there are four reasons that people monitor and measure:

- **To validate** To validate previous decisions

- **To direct** To set the direction for activities in order to meet set targets; this is the most prevalent reason for monitoring and measuring

- **To justify** To justify, with factual evidence or proof, that a course of action is required

- **To intervene** To identify a point of intervention including subsequent changes and corrective actions.

IT service providers use measurements to support a range of different activities, including:

- **Improvement planning** Monitoring and measurement is often used to establish 'Where are we now?' to justify future improvement activity, and to measure 'Did we get there?' to validate that an improvement has been effective and to intervene if it has not.

- **Detecting and reacting to events** Monitoring and measurement is at the heart of event management, enabling the IT organization to detect changes in the state of configuration items and intervene to resolve any issues detected. 'Reacting to events' does not just mean logging incidents and taking immediate technical action. For example, thresholds could be used to identify when a **service level** is in danger of being breached, and management action taken to ensure that this does not happen; the best measurement is one that is made in time to correct an issue before it impacts a customer.

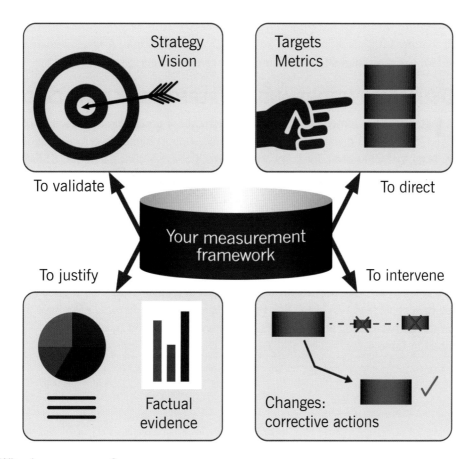

Figure 4.1 Why do we measure?

- **Reporting** All IT organizations need to produce a range of reports, which support many different activities. Service level agreement (SLA) reports for customers are used to validate that the IT organization has delivered the agreed service and to justify future improvement activities. Reports for process owners are often used to direct, ensuring that process owners focus on the correct actions, and to intervene, identifying the need for improvements. Reports can also be used to help manage suppliers, to demonstrate compliance with legal or regulatory requirements, and for many other purposes. Reporting is discussed in more detail in section 4.6.

In all of these cases, it is essential that the IT service provider measures the things that really matter.

Some organizations measure and report very large numbers of metrics, not because they are important, but because they have always measured and reported those things. Typically, many of the things that have always been measured and reported are process-focused. When new business or customer-focused metrics are put in place, the new measurements do not replace any of the existing ones, but are added to the older ones. This can result in an ever-expanding set of metrics that are too cumbersome to be of use.

Tip

A metrics review can help identify the improvements you need to ensure that you are getting real value from your measurements and reporting. Carry out a review once a year, analyse the findings, and plan improvements to ensure you are only measuring and reporting things that matter.

ITIL V3 Planning to Implement Service Management (OGC, 2010), section 6.5, reminds us that 'It is much better to select and measure a few good business- and customer-focused KPIs, rather than many general process-focused or internally focused KPIs.'

Any measurement that does not result in some kind of action is a distraction. A measurement that does not provide real value to the organization should be dropped in favour of measurements that do.

4.2 CRITICAL SUCCESS FACTORS AND KEY PERFORMANCE INDICATORS

A **critical success factor (CSF)** is something that must be achieved if an IT service, process, plan or other activity is to succeed. Section 4.3 discusses how CSFs should support higher-level goals such as the creation of customer value. Note that CSFs are *critical* success factors, not *every* success factor. CSFs should be limited to things that are critically important. Even though CSFs are important, they are often hard to measure. Examples of CSFs might be:

- **CSF1** The new IT service enables sales people to spend more time with clients
- **CSF2** Failures of the IT service do not have a significant impact on the customer's business process
- **CSF3** The company website is protected from attacks by hackers.

Each of these CSFs is important, but they might prove difficult to measure. So KPIs that can be measured need to be defined to support them. Unlike CSFs, good KPIs are actually metrics. KPIs have a number of other features that do not necessarily apply to CSFs. These are summarized by saying that KPIs should be SMART, as described in Table 4.1.

Table 4.1 The definition of SMART for KPIs

S	Specific	A specific KPI is clear, unambiguous and focused. If a KPI is not specific, then it cannot be used to validate, direct, justify or intervene.
M	Measurable	Since a KPI is a metric, it must be based on measurements. A KPI is used to assess whether something has been achieved. If it is not measurable, then it cannot be used to demonstrate achievements, judge progress, or show trends.
A	Achievable	An achievable KPI can, at least in principle, be met. If a KPI is not achievable, then it cannot assist in driving the desired behaviour. The KPI will be missed, regardless of what is done, so there is no incentive to try to achieve it.
R	Relevant	A relevant KPI helps to indicate that the CSF has been achieved. If a KPI is not relevant, then the achievement of the KPI is no indication that the CSF has been achieved.
T	Time-bound	A time-bound KPI defines the time period over which it should be measured. If a KPI is not time-bound, then it would be possible to always claim that it will be met at some ill-defined time in the future.

Table 4.2 shows some sample CSFs with associated KPIs. In each case, the suggested KPIs can be used to help demonstrate that the CSF has been achieved, but they do not prove it. That is a common feature of the relationship between CSFs and KPIs. To clarify the relationship between them, think about what the letters KPI stand for:

● **Key** The KPI helps to measure something important, not some minor aspect of what is done

● **Performance** The KPI says something about how well something is performing

● **Indicator** The KPI indicates how well something is doing, it does not prove it.

In Table 4.2, there are only two KPIs for each CSF. Sometimes as many as three or four KPIs are needed to support a CSF, but it is important to have as few as possible. If one KPI is sufficient, then just define that one; if more are needed, then make sure they really do add value. Do not give in to the temptation to measure and report more KPIs than are needed to indicate success.

The benefit of a KPI is that it can be measured, compared to a threshold or target, and used to establish trends. All of these are important. The downside is that a KPI is only an indicator of what is wanted. A very common mistake is to quote KPIs as though they are an end in themselves. It is much better to talk about CSFs, and refer to the KPIs as indicators.

Table 4.2 Examples of CSFs and associated KPIs

CSF	Associated KPIs
The new IT service enables sales people to spend more time with clients	Increase in the number of customer visits per day per sales person Sales people satisfaction survey score increased by 0.5 within 6 months
Failures of the IT service do not have a significant impact on the customer's business process	Maximum of four service outages in any year Maximum downtime of 30 minutes for any service outage
The company website is protected from attacks by hackers	Critical patches are installed on all web servers within 12 hours of notification Website penetration testing happens every 6 months

Example

A service level agreement includes the second CSF in Table 4.2 (IT failures do not impact the business), with its corresponding KPIs. When a report is delivered to the customer, it includes the KPIs, with their current values and trends, but the discussion with the customer is about the CSF.

> 'We agreed that failures of the IT service wouldn't have a significant impact on your business process. The figures we measured show that we are well within the agreed targets, and the trends are positive. Are you happy with this? Do you agree that failures didn't have a significant impact?'

This conversation uses the measured values to facilitate communication with the customer, but maintains a business focus. Many IT service providers present the KPIs to the customer and explain that the service has been good because the numbers exceed the targets, but this takes away the customer's ability to reflect on whether the service really has met their needs.

Tip

Review some of your customer reports and review meetings to see if the focus is on CSFs or KPIs. If you have been talking about the KPIs, then consider how you can change the way you present information to your customers.

Although CSFs may not be measurable, every KPI should be SMART. But even a SMART target can have unintended consequences. In addition to being SMART, it is important to review every KPI to understand how it will affect behaviour. The act of measuring something can actually result in it changing, and this is especially true when people are involved. If a KPI is used to measure people and their activities, then they will always do whatever they can to ensure that the figures look good. For example, think about what behaviour might be driven by these KPIs:

- The service desk will spend an average of two minutes or less on each phone call
- Reduced average time to find root causes of problems
- Increased percentage of services that have SLAs.

In each of the examples above, it is possible for people to improve the figures by behaving in ways that should not be encouraged. For example, if incidents are closed by the service desk within two minutes without resolving the issue, it would have been better to spend the time needed to help the user. The likelihood of this happening can be reduced by wording the KPIs carefully, but it is doubtful that it can ever be completely prevented; people who view KPIs as their targets will naturally do their best to find a way to meet them. The idea of **tension metrics** (described in *ITIL Continual Service Improvement*, section 5.5.2) can be introduced to help to ensure balanced behaviour, and this can really help to ensure that metrics drive the right behaviour.

Toolkit

More information about tension metrics can be found in section 7.2.7.

It is important though, to remember – and encourage others to remember – that KPIs are just indicators. Make sure the focus is on the CSFs that the KPIs support, rather than the KPIs in isolation. One important factor in how KPIs impact behaviour is how management makes use of the KPIs. For example, if the service desk staff get into trouble for spending more than two minutes on a phone call, this will drive particular behaviours. If instead the manager sits down with staff who take longer to understand what their challenges are and to suggest ways that they could close calls quicker, this may encourage desired behaviours.

We have already talked about the need to minimize the number of KPIs that are measured and reported; ideally there will be just one, two or three KPIs for each CSF. Of course, this means that some things will not be measured that might be important. So how to prioritize? The best solution is to base the choice of KPIs on the current maturity and effectiveness of the process or service in question, and on how this contributes value to the organization. For example, when introducing a new process, start with KPIs that show that the process is in place and starting to work. As the process improves, move to measuring how efficiently the process is working, with less emphasis on the basics. The important point is this: concentrate on KPIs in those areas where change is required, with fewer KPIs in areas where the aim is simply to maintain the current status.

4.3 METRIC CASCADES AND HIERARCHIES

Measurements and metrics cannot be created in a vacuum; they should be aligned with higher-level requirements, such as creation of value for the customer. There are a number of different ways to think about creating a hierarchy that aligns the things that are actually measured with high-level requirements. The approaches described in this section include:

● The ITIL vision-to-measurement trail
● **Balanced scorecard**
● IT component to scorecard hierarchy
● COBIT 5 goals cascade
● Organization cascade.

An approach should be chosen that is a good fit for the specific circumstances and the organizational culture, and ensure that all metrics and measurements have a higher-level purpose.

4.3.1 The ITIL vision-to-measurement trail

A metrics hierarchy starts with the vision and mission of the organization, and from these it derives goals, objectives, CSFs, KPIs, metrics and measurements (see Figure 4.2).

To define what should be measured, start by understanding the vision and mission, as described in section 3.2.1.

Next, define the goals and objectives to support the vision and mission:

● **Goals** These are expected or desired outcomes of activities or processes. For example, 'Provide reliable infrastructure to support IT services'
● **Objectives** These are targets that are necessary to achieve goals. For example, 'IT infrastructure failures do not impact the ability to meet SLA targets'.

Use each objective to identify a small number of CSFs, and for each CSF, define a small number of KPIs. The KPIs are then used to identify what measurements and metrics are needed.

> ### Example
> *To support the objective 'IT infrastructure failures do not impact the ability to meet SLA targets'*
>
> CSF: Redundancy measures ensure that services continue to operate when hardware components fail
>
> ● **KPI** Disk RAID arrays recover within 30 seconds whenever a disk fails
> ● **KPI** Replacing a failed disk drive has no impact on availability of RAID arrays.

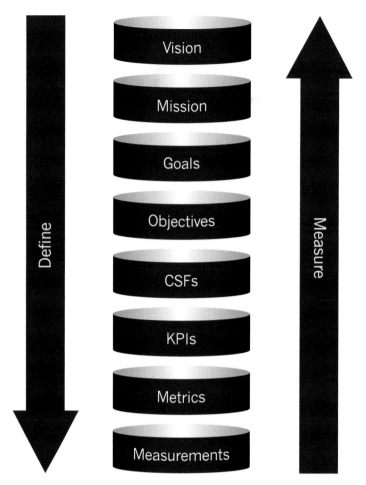

Figure 4.2 Vision-to-measurement trail

When using this approach, it is important to start defining at the very top, with the vision and mission, and then work down, ending up with the measurements. This ensures that everything measured can be tied back to the vision and mission of your organization, helping to prevent the situation where things are measured just because they can be.

When taking measurements, these cascade back up the hierarchy. The measurements are distilled into metrics, which are used to derive KPIs, which demonstrate achievements against CSFs, which help to achieve goals and objectives, and so on. Figure 4.2 shows this relationship between defining from the top down and measuring from the bottom up. The ITIL vision-to-measurement trail is further described in *ITIL Continual Service Improvement*, section 4.1.5.

Definition: Measurement

An individual piece of data about the behaviour of something of interest. For example, the date and time when one disk in RAID array KG1234 failed, or the date and time when normal service was resumed after recovery from that failure.

Definition: Metric

Something that is measured and reported to help manage a process, IT service or activity. For example, the maximum length of time taken to recover after failure of a disk in a RAID array.

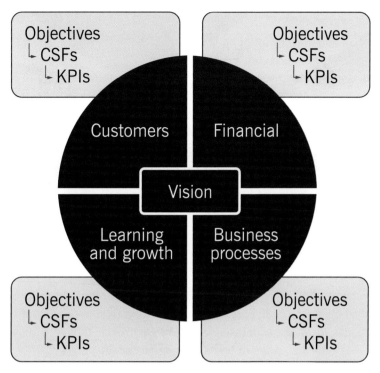

Figure 4.3 Balanced scorecard

4.3.2 Balanced scorecard

The balanced scorecard was developed by Kaplan and Norton in the mid-1990s (Kaplan and Norton, 1992). Although it was originally used for defining measurements and metrics, it has more recently been used as a framework for planning and management. It is called 'balanced' because it considers the balance between four perspectives, as shown in Table 4.3 and Figure 4.3. All of these perspectives contribute to achieving the vision and mission of the organization. Table 4.4 shows examples of CSFs aligned with a balanced scorecard.

Table 4.3 The four perspectives of the balanced scorecard

Perspective	Description
Customers	This perspective recognizes the importance of customer experience and customer satisfaction
Financial	This perspective focuses on the traditional management of finances that every organization should include
Internal (business processes)	This perspective helps to understand the health of the internal workings of the organization, and can be a good leading indicator of future performance
Innovation (learning and growth)	This perspective is closely linked to continual improvement. It includes training and development of people, management of knowledge, and other approaches that can ensure the organization is able to develop as needed

Table 4.4 Examples of CSFs aligned with segments of a balanced scorecard

Customers	Financial	Learning and growth	Business processes
Customers are satisfied with operational services	IT makes a significant contribution to business growth	IT responds rapidly to customer demand for change	End-to-end IT services are highly available
Customers are satisfied with ability to deliver new and changed services	IT makes a significant contribution to cost savings	IT staff development plans are effective	Customer incidents are resolved quickly and effectively

Defining metrics that cover all four areas of the balanced scorecard can help to ensure that there is a good balance of metrics, without too much focus on one area. At the customer level, for example, this will involve defining CSFs such as:

● **Customer satisfaction** One popular measure of satisfaction is net promoter score (NPS), which can give a quick indication of whether the needs of customers are being met. NPS is calculated by asking customers 'How likely is it that you would recommend our service to a friend or colleague?' People who give a rating of 9 or 10 (out of 10) are counted as promoters, people who give a rating of 6 or less are counted as detractors. The NPS is calculated by subtracting the percentage of detractors from the percentage of promoters.

● **Moments of truth** This could be a measurement of how well customer expectations are being met at a significant touchpoint. Identifying the key moments of truth that have the most impact on customers, and measuring how customers feel about them, can provide great insight.

These customer metrics give a very different view from traditional ITSM metrics regarding internal processes, and in combination with the other two balanced scorecard perspectives, they can help to ensure the success of the organization.

A balanced scorecard can be used at many different levels in the organization. It works best when it is used to first define very high-level objectives at the organization level, and then to cascade these down the organization structure, creating increasingly detailed targets at each level. Table 4.5 shows an example of how different targets can be defined at different levels of an organization.

Table 4.5 Examples of financial targets at different levels of an organization

Level	Target
Organization	Earnings per share
IT department	Percentage of gross revenue spent on IT
Infrastructure team	Total expenditure
Storage technician	All expenses are within policy guidelines

Targets that are defined like this can help to ensure that all metrics, measurements, KPIs, CSFs, goals and objectives throughout the organization are aligned: meeting the lower-level targets should ensure that the higher-level targets are met.

More information about the balanced scorecard can be found in *ITIL Continual Service Improvement*, section 5.5.8.

4.3.3 IT component to scorecard hierarchy

Measurements of IT components can be used to calculate service results, which can in turn be fed into an IT scorecard or a balanced scorecard. An example of this can be seen in Table 4.6.

Table 4.6 An example of an IT component to scorecard hierarchy

	Metric	Value
Component	Mainframe availability	99.96%
	WAN availability	98%
	LAN availability	97.5%
	Desktop availability	96%
Service	Service 1 availability	91.69%
	Service 2 availability	98%
Scorecard	Customer: service availability targets missed	1

The figure of 91.69% availability for Service 1 is based on the fact that this service requires all four of the listed components, so the net availability will be 99.96% × 98% × 97.5% × 96%. The availability of Service 2 is shown as 98% as this service uses the WAN, and other components that did not fail during the measurement period.

This kind of framework can be used to automate some aspects of measurement and reporting, and there are tools available to assist with this. Great care should be taken to ensure that the results actually match the customers' experience of the service. Good IT metrics should focus on customer value creation, considering things such as user productivity, amount of product sold or other business-focused measures. It is also important to measure more qualitative aspects of customer experience such as NPS and moments of truth (see section 4.3.2). Just because a measurement produces a convincing-looking number does not mean that customers care about it. Every time something is measured, think about it from a systems view. Think about what it means in terms of the end-to-end creation of value for the customer, not just in terms of the specific component. ITIL defines a system as a number of related things that work together to achieve an overall objective, and it is the overall objective that we care about, not the performance of the individual parts.

More information about a component to scorecard hierarchy can be found in *ITIL Continual Service Improvement*, section 5.4.2.

4.3.4 COBIT 5 goals cascade

COBIT 5 is a business framework for the governance and management of enterprise IT, which is maintained and published by ISACA. One element of this framework is a goals cascade that defines goals at a number of different levels. This goals cascade describes how enterprise goals are based on stakeholder needs (and stakeholder drivers) and how these in turn cascade to IT-related goals and then to enabler goals (COBIT enablers are policies, processes, infrastructure etc.).

The key point to note is that each process metric can be traced all the way through the goals cascade to understand how it contributes to shareholder needs.

Toolkit

An example of a COBIT goals cascade can be found in section 7.2.8.

4.3.5 Organization cascade

Every organization measures performance at multiple levels. This typically includes metrics for the following:

- Organization
- Business unit
- Department
- Team
- Person.

Even if none of the other approaches described in section 4.3 has been adopted, metrics and measurements will still need to be defined at all the levels that apply to the circumstances.

When defining goals, bear in mind that if they are to be effective, goals should not be arbitrary. Goals for a person should be designed to support the goals of the team that person is a member of. Similarly, the goals of the team should be designed to support the goals of the department, departmental goals should support the goals of the business unit, and the goals of all business units should support the overall organizational goals.

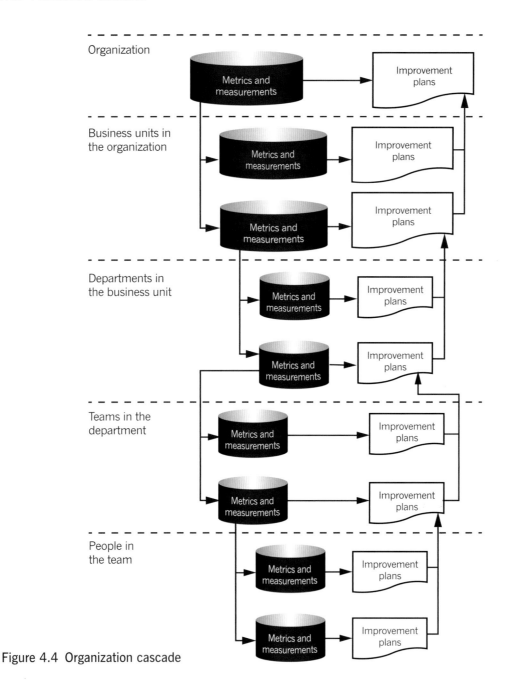

Figure 4.4 Organization cascade

When measuring and reporting at multiple levels, identify improvement opportunities at each level, too. Moreover, well-defined metrics can contribute to an entire hierarchy of improvement plans, each of which will contribute to improvement at all levels, not just at its own level. Figure 4.4 shows how measurement at each level can drive improvement plans at the same level as well as measurement at the level below, and how improvement plans at each level can feed up to higher-level improvement plans.

Note that a single metric or measurement at a higher level is often supported by multiple metrics and measurements at the next lower level. Similarly, improvement plans at a higher level may be supported by many lower-level improvement plans. It can be helpful to think of this as an iterative approach, with metrics defined at each level to support higher-level metrics, and improvement plans at each level supporting higher-level improvement plans. Figure 4.4 shows just two lower-level metrics and improvement plans for each one at a higher level, but in practice there could be many more.

Tip
Organizations that do not understand how to align goals can easily become dysfunctional, with different groups working towards goals that conflict or focusing on group goals that are not actually contributing to the overall needs of the organization.

4.4 METRIC CATEGORIES

Less really can be more when it comes to metrics and measurement. But that will only be the case provided everything important has in fact been taken into account. Categorizing metrics and measurements can help to ensure that there is a suitable balance across a number of different categories.

In the balanced scorecard, there is an example which used four categories: customers; financial; business processes; learning and growth. This section describes a number of other ways that metrics and measurements can be categorized. These include:

- Technology, process and service
- Progress, compliance, effectiveness and efficiency
- Leading and trailing
- Inside-out and outside-in.

It is very useful to think about these four sets of categories when creating metrics, as each set focuses on a different, but important, aspect that needs to be measured.

4.4.1 Technology, process and service metrics

It is important to collect metrics that help in understanding the performance of technology, processes and services:

- **Technology metrics** These capture data about infrastructure and applications; for example, the availability or performance of a server or network, or the workload measured at a firewall
- **Process metrics** These are used to help understand how well individual ITSM processes are working; for example, the average time for a technical support group to accept escalated incidents, or the time taken by the network team to provide additional bandwidth when requested
- **Service metrics** These are a measure of the end-to-end service performance; for example, the availability of an end-to-end service, the average time to resolve Priority 1 incidents, or the average number of business transactions carried out every minute. Service metrics should enable you to answer questions about the value, outcomes, costs and risks (VOCR) of the service.

When designing IT services, consider not only the end-to-end services that you want to deliver, but also how the processes and technology contribute to these. If you only measure the end-to-end services then you will have a very limited understanding of why the services are performing the way they are, or what you can do to make improvements. It is essential to collect all three types of metric so that you can understand how your services are performing, and why.

It can be surprisingly easy to miscategorize a metric. For example, a metric such as percentage availability could refer to either the technology or the service, depending on what is measured. In this case, customer reports could be providing technology metrics, while what the customer really wants to know about is the end-to-end service. This can result in miscommunication, with the service provider claiming to have achieved a KPI and the customer confused and dissatisfied.

Customers are, generally, much less interested in technology and process metrics than in service metrics, because they care most about how well the service meets their needs. When a customer starts to ask pointed questions about technology or process metrics, this can be a warning; it may mean that they are not happy with the service and have lost confidence in the service provider.

More information about technology, process and service metrics can be found in *ITIL Continual Service Improvement*, section 5.5.

4.4.2 Progress, compliance, effectiveness and efficiency metrics

Processes and services can be measured using the four different types of metric shown in Table 4.7.

Table 4.7 Types of process metrics

Metric	Description
Progress	Milestones and deliverables in the capability of a process or service. Typically actions completed or percentage project completion. For example, 'The new service has undergone external penetration testing' or '90% of staff have been trained in the new incident management process'
Compliance	Compliance with governance and regulatory requirements, or with the use of a process. A compliance metric is often a simple pass/fail or yes/no. For example, 'An external penetration test has been carried out every six months'
Effectiveness	How well the process delivers the required results. For example, 'Number of vulnerabilities identified during external penetration tests'
Efficiency	How well the process uses resources. For example, 'Average cost of external penetration testing'

The maturity and status of a process should help to determine the type of measurement and metric you should use. For a new process, look at progress metrics (what is in place, what is still needed?) and compliance metrics (are people doing what they should to meet governance and regulatory requirements?). As the process becomes more mature, your emphasis should move to effectiveness metrics (are we getting the required outputs?) and finally to efficiency. If you start monitoring efficiency too early, it can have negative consequences. It takes time for a process to become efficient, and trying to make changes in the name of efficiency before the process has time to become embedded may make it harder for the process to become effective.

As efficiency and effectiveness metrics are added, gradually reduce the number of progress and compliance metrics to avoid the problem of measuring so many things that any reports become unusable.

> ### Example: Metrics for a new process
>
> If you are introducing a new service portfolio management process, you could start with progress metrics, such as 'Policy has been approved by IT and business management' or '20 services are listed in the service portfolio with information about their cost and value'. Later you may add an effectiveness metric such as 'The service portfolio provides the information needed when writing business cases for new or changed services', and finally efficiency metrics related to the amount of time and effort needed to maintain the service portfolio.

More information about progress, compliance, effectiveness and efficiency metrics can be found in *ITIL Service Design*, section 3.7.5.

4.4.3 Leading and trailing metrics

Metrics can help you understand past performance and predict what is yet to come. Categorizing metrics as 'leading' and 'trailing' can help ensure the right balance between understanding and learning from the past and planning for the future.

● **Trailing metrics** Often referred to as lag indicators, these tell you about what has been achieved. For example, if you measure and report average time to resolve Priority 2 incidents, it tells you what was achieved last month and last quarter. This figure may appear in your SLA reports, but while you may also use it to help report trends, it is basically information about what has already happened.

- **Leading metrics** These help to predict what might happen in the future. For example, if you measure and report the percentage of Priority 2 incidents that are not being actively worked on, this can help you to predict what figures to expect in next month's SLA report.

Customers are often interested in the trailing metrics, and this is what you should report to them. However, you should also collect and use the leading metrics that will help you to achieve your targets in the future.

4.4.4 Inside-out and outside-in metrics

Outside-in measurement is an idea that comes from business management, but it has great value in understanding IT. The distinction between outside-in and inside-out is that an outside-in view of an IT service looks at everything you do from a customer perspective, whereas an inside-out view is an IT service provider perspective. Whenever you design a process, or plan an improvement, you should always take an outside-in approach, ensuring that what you create is based on understanding how customers will use, perceive and get value from what you do.

This can also be applied to metrics:

- **Outside-in metrics** Represent the customers' view of IT services. Every customer-facing report should be based on outside-in metrics, which are about the things customers want and need.
- **Inside-out metrics** Represent the internal IT view of services. You may need some inside-out metrics to help your process managers or technical teams understand the internal workings of IT, but these should always be considered in the context of how they ultimately impact customers.

Example: Inside-out and outside-in metrics

An organization deploys a new customer relationship management (CRM) system, which is intended to help it manage information about customers. Here are three different metrics they could measure to understand availability of the service:

- Percentage availability of the servers, network and storage
- Percentage availability of the end-to-end CRM system
- Percentage of customer appointments where the salesperson has information about the customer in time for them to read and understand it.

The first two are inside-out metrics, based on thinking about IT. The third is an outside-in metric, based on thinking about the ability of the customer to use the CRM system to create value.

4.4.5 Using categories

To gain insight into how well balanced the metrics are, make sure that every metric collected is categorized using all four sets of categories. For example, one metric might be categorized as an inside-out leading indicator of process compliance, whereas another might be an outside-in trailing indicator of service effectiveness.

Looking at the metrics and thinking about these categories can help to ensure that nothing has been missed that should be measured, and that there is a good balance without too many metrics in any one area. Table 4.8 shows how some example metrics could be categorized, using the four different categories described in this publication.

A visual summary of the categories covered by the metrics, expressed in a simple table format such as Table 4.8, can help to identify whether or not they are balanced, and if they are not, which metrics are missing, and which could be eliminated.

Table 4.8 Example categorization of KPIs

	Technology/ process/service	Progress/ compliance/ effectiveness/ efficiency	Leading/trailing	Inside-out/outside-in
Percentage end-to-end service availability	Service	Effectiveness	Trailing	Inside-out
Average percentage utilization of servers	Technology	Efficiency	Trailing	Inside-out
Number of problems with tested workarounds	Process	Effectiveness	Leading	Inside-out
Percentage of customer appointments where the salesperson has information about the customer	Service	Effectiveness	Trailing	Outside-in

4.5 ASSESSMENTS

Assessments can be used to measure, analyse and understand the behaviour and performance of processes, services, technology, people, or anything else that needs to be understood. An assessment involves taking measurements, comparing these to expectations, making a judgement about them and documenting everything learned in a report. Every assessment should have a clear purpose, and should support the creation of value for customers.

A good assessment will not just identify gaps and issues, but will also identify things that are being done well that need to be built on. Identifying what people are doing wrong and asking them to change may have some effect, but also identifying what they are doing well and encouraging them to do more of that, and to spread those good practices to other areas, can be much more effective.

An assessment can be based on a one-off capture of information at a point in time, or it can be part of a regular programme designed to understand how capabilities are evolving over time. Before starting to plan an assessment, make sure that you fully understand its purpose. Typical examples of the purpose of an assessment might be:

● To understand how well one or more processes are working

● To establish a baseline for measuring future improvement activity

● To understand how well an improvement project has progressed

● To compare how work is done in multiple locations prior to creating a new consolidated approach

● To find out how much effort would be needed to comply with a standard such as ISO/IEC 20000

● To compare the service provision with alternatives that the customers might consider.

Whatever the purpose, document it and ensure that all stakeholders have a common understanding of what you are trying to achieve. Without this, it will be extremely hard to run an effective assessment and it is likely that the output generated will not match your needs.

Many aspects of an assessment could be delivered by a third party, but defining the purpose and scope is something that you need to do yourself. When considering whether to engage a third party, consider:

● Do you have the skills, experience and resources needed to carry out the assessment yourself?

● Do you have sufficient independence that you can offer a fair assessment? Most people will overestimate their own capability and competence.

● Do you have sufficient credibility within your organization that the findings of the assessment will be accepted?

● Do you have an independent team within your own organization who could carry out an assessment for you?

- Do you have access to suitable assessment criteria?
- What is the cost of engaging a third party compared with doing the assessment yourself?
- Do you need external benchmark data that could be provided by a third party?

4.5.1 Assessment scope

The scope of the assessment should be no more than is needed to achieve your purpose. An assessment with a very broad scope can be extremely expensive and time consuming. An assessment with a very narrow scope may not deliver the information required. An assessment with a poorly defined scope is likely to waste significant time and resources collecting the wrong data.

Even if your assessment is part of a regular series of assessments, the scope of each specific assessment still needs to be considered. Requirements can change over time, perhaps because a rolling programme of assessments is run that looks at different aspects, or maybe because your needs have changed since the previous assessment.

Before the scope of an assessment can be agreed, make sure all the stakeholders have been identified, and that your ability to influence the situation being assessed is understood. The orientation worksheet is a good starting point to help with this.

There is nothing wrong with carrying out an assessment to understand, for example, incident management delivered by a single service desk, if that is what is needed. Equally, an assessment of just one service delivered to a single customer could be carried out, but include all the processes, infrastructure, applications, support teams and suppliers involved in delivering that service. What is important is that the scope defined is able to meet the purpose of the assessment, and that all the different factors have been considered.

Toolkit
Section 7.2.6.5 provides an assessment planning worksheet to help with defining the scope of an assessment. See also the orientation worksheet in section 7.1.2.

4.5.2 Assessment criteria

The success of an assessment depends in part on ensuring that the right questions are asked and the right data is collected. There are a number of possible sources of assessment frameworks; each of these sources covers a different scope, and has a different design philosophy. Choosing which is required depends on the purpose and scope of the assessment. What is essential is to ensure that there are well-defined criteria, closely matched to the purpose and scope of the assessment.

Toolkit
Section 7.2.5 includes a list of sources for frameworks and criteria that should be considered when planning an assessment. A combination of these may need to be used, and additional criteria may need to be included to assess technology components or any other area that is within your scope but not covered by one of these frameworks.

4.5.3 Assessment outputs

When planning an assessment, consider what outputs are required. The data collection should be managed to ensure all the outputs needed to cover the scope and purpose of the assessment are able to be generated. The outputs will typically be presented in graphical form, with attendant text.

Toolkit

Section 7.2 gives examples of some typical graphical outputs of assessments, including the ITIL Maturity Model.

Typical assessment outputs are described in Table 4.9.

Table 4.9 Examples of assessment outputs

Gap analysis	Differences between actual practice and the chosen assessment criteria
SWOT analysis	Identification of strengths, weaknesses, opportunities and **threat**s
Process metrics	Process achievements expressed in numerical terms
Process maturity	An estimation of the process maturity based on a tool such as the ITIL Process Maturity Model. It is important to note that process maturity is not a reliable indicator of the value of a process, and care should be taken when measuring and reporting this
Organization maturity	An estimation of the maturity of the overall organization
Change readiness	An estimation of the ability of the organization to transition to a new way of working
Customer satisfaction	A measurement of how customers and users feel about the services
SLA achievement	A comparison of service performance against SLA targets
Benchmark comparison	A comparison of the results of this assessment with the results of similar assessments carried out for other comparable organizations

A more detailed discussion of benchmarking can be found in *ITIL Continual Service Improvement*, section 5.3. *ITIL Service Design*, Appendix H, goes deeper into process maturity frameworks.

4.6 REPORTING

After collecting measurements, there is a lot of work to do. The data will need to be assembled and analysed to extract value. This value could take any of the forms identified in section 4.1 (to validate, direct, justify or intervene).

Decide how to present the results. This involves identifying all the relevant stakeholders, and making sure each stakeholder's needs are understood. Presentation of metrics and measurements is usually done by means of reports and dashboards:

● Reports provide a considered summary and analysis of metrics. As described in section 4.1, they may be used to validate, direct, justify or intervene.

  Typically a report will present the data that was collected, compare it with thresholds to establish whether KPIs have been met, analyse it to show trends and exceptions, and finally include recommendations as to what action should follow on from the analysis.

● Dashboards provide a quick visual summary of metrics. They are often created by ITSM tools and are typically updated very frequently, so that the current status can always be seen. They can show the status of technology (applications and infrastructure availability), of processes (service desk queue length) or of end-to-end services (number of successful and failed transactions in the last hour).

  Dashboards are often used to facilitate rapid intervention (when a threshold is exceeded), but they can also be used to validate, by showing that everything is normal. Dashboards should be created for specific audiences; the information needed by the service desk manager is very different from that needed by a business unit manager.

4.6.1 Improving the value of reports

Many IT service providers create reports with no clear purpose, and no identified stakeholders, and some produce reports that provide very little value. These organizations could often save time and effort if they simply stopped producing such reports.

Some IT departments produce long reports full of data that is never read. These reports are often based on requests made by management many years ago, but the managers who requested the reports have moved on and nobody ever looks at them. In other IT departments, there are reports with hundreds of data items, but only three or four of them are ever used.

To make sure that reports create the maximum value, always ask:

● Who is the report for?

   Make sure the intended audience is known for each report created. Then talk to those people and ask if they actually want the report, what they use it for, and which parts of it they use. If an audience for the report cannot be identified, then think about not creating it any more. If the audience only use some of the data in the report, then consider cutting it down to just the data they need.

● What is the purpose of the report?

   If a report does not have a clear purpose, then it almost certainly contains unnecessary data. If it is not known what a report is for and the audience for that report cannot identify what it is used for, then stop creating it.

● What is being done as a result of the report, and who is doing it?

   Remember that the purpose of metrics and measurement is to validate, direct, justify or intervene. Find out which of these is happening as a result of the report. If the data is simply being ignored, then consider not creating it. Before creating a new report, a clear action plan should be devised for it, specifying who will get the report and what they will do with it each time they receive it. The purpose of every report should be to provide the evidence needed to make good decisions based on understanding risk, value, cost or some other important attribute of the thing being measured.

   Even if the report is being used, make sure it is making a definite contribution to the goals or objectives of your organization. If it is not, then discuss the value with the report recipient and see if it can be fixed; otherwise it makes sense to stop producing the report.

● What data is needed to create the report?

   Most measurements are created to contribute to reports, so it is a good idea to analyse the metrics and measurements from this point of view. For example, there may be hundreds of different categories for incidents, which have been created over the years at the request of colleagues or customers in order for them to distinguish between them. This large number of categories can make the incident management process inefficient, causing delays when service desk agents are logging incidents. If all the service desk reports are reviewed with the stakeholders who use them, it may be found that not only can the reports be simplified but, as a result, the categories on the service desk can be simplified. Similarly, financial reports may be created based on categories that were needed many years ago, but are no longer suitable. Reports should always be discussed with the relevant stakeholders to understand what they really need, and then ensure the right data is collected to support their requirements.

When designing reports, bear in mind that a picture can be much more powerful than words. Try to use charts, graphs and diagrams instead of large amounts of text and numbers. Additional discussion of reports can be found in *ITIL Continual Service Improvement*, section 5.5.6.

Toolkit

Section 7.2.6 provides examples of assessment report content.

4.7 CONTINUAL IMPROVEMENT OF METRICS AND MEASUREMENT

Like everything else in ITSM, metrics and measurement should be subject to continual improvement. Changes may be needed to what is measured, what thresholds and KPIs are set, or how you report, based on many things, including:

● New or changed business processes

● Changes to regulatory or governance requirements

● New or changed IT services

● New or changed infrastructure or applications

● Increased maturity or effectiveness of existing processes

● Changes to organizational structure or reporting lines

● Results of previous improvement activities.

This means that metrics and reporting need to be considered when any of these criteria change. In addition, every metric, KPI, CSF and report should be reviewed at least annually to ensure that it is still fulfilling its intended purpose. Without this, more and more measurements and reporting will be added, without removing the overhead of metrics and reports that are no longer needed.

To sum up, metrics and measurement are an essential part of managing IT services, but they are only useful if the right things are being measured, for the right reasons. The most important idea when thinking about metrics is to measure what matters, and take action based on what has been measured.

5

Communication

This chapter covers:

- Why good communication is important
- Communication principles
- Communication techniques

5 Communication

5.1 WHY GOOD COMMUNICATION IS IMPORTANT

The quality of communication between people is a major contributor to the success, or failure, of most endeavours. Being able to communicate successfully and effectively is a key business skill, without which there is no guarantee that teams or individuals within the organization are working to the same goals, or that they even know what each other is doing.

Good communication is not just about being human or nice, although that helps. Good communication is about being efficient, responsive, professional and effective, ideally in an environment of trust, transparency and mutual respect. This is done by recognizing and actively responding to the intellectual and emotional needs of those with whom we interact. The process of engaging and involving people and recognizing and using their feedback is an important factor in the success of any service or project.

Communication is more than simply sending and receiving messages. Communication needs a goal, as demonstrated in the following examples:

- Discover customer/user needs
- Discover business requirements and priorities
- Understand the workings and objectives of other teams and stakeholders
- Provide influence, inspiration and motivation
- Develop and maintain synergy with other teams and customers
- Receive and deliver clear information and instructions
- Manage expectations
- Identify and respond to progress
- Recover from difficult situations
- Build and maintain successful partnerships and relationships
- Deliver, receive and accept feedback
- Promote success
- Confirm and demonstrate commitment.

5.1.1 Communication and ITSM

Communication is fundamental to success in IT service management (ITSM). Poor communication can ruin good plans, and can lead to waste and inefficiency through unnecessary costs, delays and poor service delivery, as well as through the disruption and distraction of disagreement. A team might build a perfect set of ITIL processes and tools, but these will be of little value unless enough has been done to ensure they are followed and used by the relevant people.

Processes and initiatives do not succeed by themselves. They need people to inspire and drive others to make them happen. They also need people to be smart and to react quickly when there are gaps and potential issues. Good communication enables this to happen.

Key message

All teams need clear communication around operational plans. For example, sports teams need to be clear on the proposed tactics, otherwise team members will have different approaches and their opposition will exploit their weakness. Players need to be inspired and motivated to engage and participate with 100% commitment, and they also need information on what is happening in the game.

Leaders must be able to explain and team members must also be able to understand what is expected of them. Successful, timely and effective communication can be the difference between winning and losing a game.

5.1.2 Examples of effective communication

- Providing clear information around expected ways of working, i.e. following processes
- Using a variety of tools and media to disseminate a single message across an organization
- Clarifying business impact and urgency of incidents when escalating to other teams
- Checking that processes and work instructions are understood
- Speeding up the delivery of new services
- Agreeing expectations of service delivery with customers
- Confirming the actual level of customer satisfaction with a service
- Agreeing and following escalation processes
- Understanding and committing to change as part of a continual service improvement (CSI) approach
- Agreeing call-back times to follow up incidents with a customer
- Demonstrating to staff how to deal professionally with customers
- Driving activity to resolve incidents and problems, and coordinating the people responsible
- Achieving on-time and in-budget delivery as a result of teamwork and clear goals
- Clarifying impact and urgency and outcomes as part of service level agreement (SLA) negotiations
- Keeping customers and management informed of progress with issues
- Providing and disseminating steps that will be followed as part of a workaround.

5.1.3 Key benefits of good communication

In simple terms, good communication goes a long way to ensuring that services and processes run smoothly, on time, on budget, as expected and with minimum disruption or delay.

The key benefits that can be expected from good communication include:

- Increased efficiency and cost optimization through optimum synergy and teamwork. Many initiatives run over budget and with high waste, often caused by missed expectations, missed deadlines and high cost of duplication and rework. Much of this can be caused by failures of understanding and exchange of information, particularly around logistics.
- Speedier service delivery and issue resolution due to increased transparency and understanding of service priorities. Positive working environments tend to be more stable and with less frequent changes in personnel.
- Positive working culture. Good communication means a positive working environment, with a close working understanding between people and teams. This can lead to greater innovation, integration, creativity and a shared desire to improve.

- A positive and trusting working culture that supports more flexible and open ways of working, and an openness to new ideas and opportunities. Often people are hesitant to make suggestions or raise issues or risks if they feel that this might reflect badly on them if they fail. A transparent and supportive organization, based on personal trust between people across all levels, encourages and expects people to come up with new ideas and to feel comfortable about experimenting and suggesting new ideas for improvement.

- Improved credibility, resulting from an organization that is authentic and transparent, and where people feel that they can be open and honest with each other and share ideas and experiences. Issues will surface more easily in this environment and the positive force of teamwork will usually help to resolve them more quickly. This is frequently visible outside the organization and can be a positive PR and marketing advantage, as well as improving customer, and possibly market, confidence.

5.1.4 Issues caused by poor communication

Misunderstandings usually result in the need to re-visit work, which in turn means delay and added cost. For example:

- **Unmet customer needs** If the deliverables of an initiative do not meet requirements, due to missed expectations, this causes delay, dissatisfaction and additional cost. Often this can be the result of poor requirements gathering with the customer, plus inadequate clarification and iteration of initial documentation from the service provider.

- **Delays and missed deadlines** If deadlines for an initiative and service delivery are missed due to lack of clear and SMART (specific, measurable, achievable, relevant and time-bound) agreements and objectives, or if customer requirements have not been properly defined and confirmed, and then qualified in realistic and practical terms, incorrect assumptions and wasted development can result.

- **Customer dissatisfaction** This can happen when the customer is unhappy with delivery while the service provider thinks they are doing a good job meeting what are, in effect, inadequate targets. Poorly defined SLAs can lead to a relationship divide between the service provider and customer, which is often referred to as the watermelon SLA effect, i.e. it looks green on the outside but is red inside.

- **Unnecessary expense and customer delays** If progress updates and messages fail to get across the two or three key points that actually matter, which may be lost in documentation that is poorly written or contains superfluous detail, this wastes time and also fails to deliver what is needed to update relevant stakeholders on progress. This can cause delay and waste through misunderstanding.

- **Avoidably slow restoration of service** If incidents are escalated beyond the service desk without suitable classification on business impact or agreed processes between teams, there may be a situation where two support analysts assume that the other is working on the same incident, although neither is. The customer waits for their service to be restored, but no one is working on it.

- **Wasted time and rework** When IT issues occur, technical people sometimes make assumptions about the work their colleagues are doing, without checking what is really happening. Less technical people who have people skills may reach out to their colleagues to ensure the work is being covered. This can come down to the levels of comfort and drive that individuals have to contact their colleagues in other teams. The net effect is the potential for wasted time and wasted work.

- **Inability to improve services** This can happen when improvement activities do not happen as expected due to resistance and lack of understanding. People work better together, and want to do so, when they have a good relationship. The better the quality of the relationship between individuals and groups, and the more complete the shared understanding, the simpler it is to negotiate and work together to change things.

- **Inefficiency** It is easier to deal with resistance if there is a basis of personal understanding between people. Lack of understanding can lead to inefficiency and poor staff morale.

- **The 'black hole' syndrome** The black hole syndrome happens when an incident or other issue is escalated beyond the initial point of contact, and through lack of communication it disappears from the customer/user view into a void of silence. Maybe the issue has not been acknowledged and needs to be owned. Maybe the incident has been picked up and is being actioned, yet there is no communication to give an update on developments. When the customer calls to find out what is happening, there is a rush of activity to find information, which wastes time and delays feedback. The service desk may be hesitant to call the necessary team as there is not a good relationship in place and this adds to delay in feedback, as well as prolonging the time taken to resolve the incident.

A poor communication culture can also lead to instability, low morale and high staff turnover, as well as loss of customer confidence, which may have serious financial implications. We need to develop good communication skills if we want to be successful, particularly in collaborative and customer-facing work.

Example

An external vendor is scheduled to deliver key technical skills and activities on-site on predefined days. The buying organization does not schedule the appropriate people to be available on these days for system access. These expensive resources have to sit around doing nothing all day, costing money and delaying progress.

This may have happened because of a lack of clarity and explanation from either side, with too many assumptions about who was doing what and no checking or confirmation that diaries were in sync. However the upshot is unnecessary delay and cost, which could have been avoided if clear proactive and transparent communication had taken place.

5.1.5 ITSM considerations

ITSM organizations have evolved organically, based around technologies and key technical areas. As a result, the structure of many traditional IT organizations does not reflect the way that IT services are consumed and experienced by users.

What ITIL aims to do with integrated processes is to pull together these structures into a single functional supply chain that has clearly defined ownership and delivery responsibility. Inevitably, there will be issues and questions around who owns or is responsible for dealing with specific work, particularly when this might cross the boundaries of respective technical teams.

This is why good communication is essential for ITSM, optimizing strong relationships and building shared goals between teams and individuals in order to deliver a joined-up service.

In ITSM, effective communication is particularly important for several reasons:

- IT organizations are still relatively new and evolving, compared to most departments and disciplines. Many people have different ideas of how to make this work. The 'adopt and adapt' approach requires agreement and clarification in each organization.

- ITSM requires cooperation and collaboration. People and teams need to work together with clear common goals. Collaboration requires strong relationships, built on trust and mutual understanding across all teams and functional areas: service desk and IT support teams; operations and development; staff and management; IT; and so on, through the organization. Good communication and relationship–building helps to break down these barriers.

- Change is a constant. Currency and accuracy of information are essential. Up-to-date information must be clearly, securely and regularly communicated to those who need it.

- Projects involving services are prone to changing requirements and misunderstanding between stakeholders. These issues are best resolved quickly and this happens naturally when there are strong positive relationships and communication channels.

- The more traditional ad hoc IT culture is giving way to a more demanding customer base and expectation levels. IT users are more demanding and IT-literate, with a need for more consistency, transparency and quality from IT organizations, and little regard for who actually delivers the service.

- Communication is a vital ingredient when dealing with processes and tools. Dealing with the human side of processes can go a long way towards ensuring their success.

There should be little doubt around the value and benefit of including and focusing on communication as a key element in any ITSM initiative. This requires a different set of skills and competencies from technical or process knowledge and experience. These additional skills are of equal importance to the more technical know-how.

Any professional organization wishing to use ITSM for business quality and improvement – large or small, regardless of industry or geography – must embrace the need to deliver successful and effective communication.

All people involved in delivering or receiving a service, from the CIO to a junior analyst, have a responsibility to ensure that their inter-personal communication skills are as effective as possible. Communication is not simply one person's or one team's responsibility. It is an imperative for everyone in the working environment.

Systems and services will inevitably fail at the weakest point. Often this happens as a result of missed expectations or incomplete escalation and communications processes.

It is not realistic or sensible to have a process for everything, so effective and productive human interaction and exchange of communication are required to ensure that processes and service delivery actually work.

5.2 COMMUNICATION PRINCIPLES

Some people are naturally better at communicating than others. However, even people who do not consider they have good communication skills can benefit from understanding the fundamentals of communication.

The principles required for good communication can be summarized as follows:

- Communication is a two-way process
- We are all communicating, all the time
- Timing and frequency matter
- There is no single method of communicating that works for everyone
- The message is in the medium.

It is important to bear these principles in mind when presenting information. Understanding the audience, being aware of differing communication styles, and considering timing, medium and mode of distribution will all help to ensure collaborations are successful.

Tips

Human communication has a lot in common with IT communication protocols.

As soon as computers began to communicate with one another, simple protocols were required to establish that contact was reliable, consistent and two-way. Most electronic communication is based on the following:

- Making contact – verifying and acknowledging the link. This happens as a two-way process, with send and acknowledgement messages being exchanged.
- Maintaining contact – ensuring that the contact remains in place and that messages are exchanged successfully. This involves a continual process of send/ acknowledgement messages.

Technology communication protocols do the things that humans often forget to do:

- Check and acknowledge that contact has been made
- Keep checking and verifying the contact.

If no acknowledgement has been received then the sender needs to take further action to re-establish the connection or use another means to send the message.

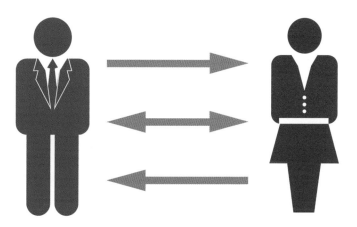

Figure 5.1 Communication is a two-way process

5.2.1 Communication is a two-way process

Communication happens all the time. People constantly act as both sender and receiver. Communication is not simply sending out a message; that is broadcasting. Communication is multi-lateral, pervasive, duplex and constant (Figure 5.1).

The sender cannot assume that, just because they have sent a message, it has been received and understood. There is a reason that the message was sent. It is the responsibility of the sender to ensure that the required outcome has been achieved. The receiver also has a responsibility to check and confirm that what has been sent to them is correctly understood.

Simply sending out an email is not enough to complete a communication. It is imperative that the sender is aware that their message has been sent, and that the recipient has received and understood it.

It is useful to employ checks and tests to ascertain whether the underlying message has been absorbed. This can be done through a variety of methods varying from formal checks to informal chats in passing while grabbing a coffee. With larger initiatives, it is useful to collect data on the most successful communication media, so as to optimize future communication.

5.2.1.1 ITSM considerations

- Delays can cost customers downtime and goodwill, so proactive communication may be needed to ensure that escalations work effectively. Many issues in ITSM are caused because one team has sent another team a ticket, and assumes that to be the end of their involvement. Escalations should always be tracked and checked upon.

- Processes and tasks do not complete themselves. Just because something is written on a plan with a person's name against it, that does not guarantee it gets done. Service managers have a responsibility to not only send out updates but also to chase for updates and actions, as well as checking that participants have an accurate understanding of what is expected of them.

- When meeting with users and customers to discuss requirements, SLAs and services, it is essential that IT professionals do not do all the talking. The meeting is an opportunity to understand the customer's experience and to provide assurance that their experience is understood by IT. It is unwise to offer solutions without listening first. A key component of human interaction is to acknowledge that another party's perspective is understood. This builds trust and helps to foster a constructive and effective relationship.

- It is important to clearly define the stakeholders involved in delivering and receiving a service. The different stakeholders will each have different needs which can be best met if their position and preferred communication channels are understood. For example, a service review with a customer might need a simple one-page report and a monthly telephone call, whereas an internal project review may need a project plan update and project governance, discussed at a face-to-face meeting.

● It is vital that communication should be proactive and multi-lateral, not just reactive and unilateral. Two-way conversation improves the chance of understanding what people think and how they respond to information sent to them or what is expected from them. Listening and observing are key communications skills that have a big impact on successful collaboration. It is useful to see how other individuals and teams work. By sitting in on their meetings and listening to what they say, the opportunity is there to build appropriate and workable solutions.

5.2.2 We are all communicating, all of the time

We are constantly conveying messages (Figure 5.2), through body language, tone of voice or even by omission. For example, we can make a statement about how we consider particular individuals by leaving them out of a meeting or email trail.

There are various statistics regarding the extent to which actual communication – that is, successful transfer of relevant information – is delivered non-verbally. There are claims that the most important element is not what is said but how it is expressed. Regardless, non-verbal communication should be taken seriously as a major critical success factor (CSF).

People who are understood to be good communicators are considered to have high emotional intelligence which allows them to read people. Communication requires an acknowledgement of the emotional state of the person who is being communicated with. Successful communication involves being flexible enough to use appropriate content and tone in order to achieve the desired objective.

It is useful to consider what might be called stage management when progressing large initiatives, such as big projects. This includes a consideration of what message is to be conveyed. For example, by running a workshop attended by key stakeholders within the project, the project is given the stakeholder's tacit support.

At an operational level, the concept of setting the tone in a team is useful. This might mean, for example, reflecting the demographic of the customer base in the diversity of the people who work on the service desk. It is important that the team is able to empathize with their customers, who are more likely to get in contact if they feel comfortable.

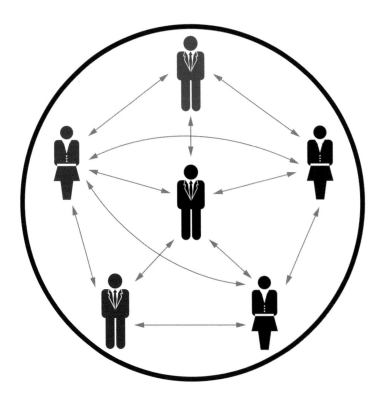

Figure 5.2 We are all communicating, all of the time

At a personal level, people should be aware of their own communication style and how this might positively or negatively impact on other co-workers and stakeholders. Are they seen as a listener and inclusive worker, or do they coerce people to their point of view through force of character? Successful project managers and change agents need to have a portfolio of communications techniques and approaches in order to get the best results.

5.2.2.1 ITSM considerations

● ITSM, by its nature, entails collaboration between a large and disparate group of stakeholders, including customers, users, service desk, IT teams and managers. Each of these will form an opinion about the value of ITSM. It is important to be cognizant of this in all activities and communication. Each stakeholder can be engaged by, for example, actively soliciting feedback.

● When implementing ITSM tools and processes across the IT department, ensure that messages to stakeholders are simple, short and to the point. Key points may get lost within excessive extraneous information or hefty manuals. Concise communication shows the stakeholder's time is valued. Such consideration will smooth the collaboration.

● Service desks are often the public face of an organization. The way the service desk interacts with users has a very high impact on the users' image of the whole organization. The quality of the service desk team, and the escalated support it gets from other teams, can determine the organization's perceived business value to customers. IT workers similarly create an image of their team in their colleagues' and customers' minds. They should be aware of the need to be professional and positive in their interactions.

Example

At an initiative meeting for a new set of ITSM processes, tools and changes to ways of working, a technical support team leader agrees to support the initiative and work to a new set of procedures and work instructions. He had previously shown resistance to the changes. The team assumes that he has had a change of heart and is now an active supporter of the changes.

At lunch, he is heard to discuss the initiative with other staff in a patronizing and cynical way, saying 'Yes, we all need to follow these new processes'. His tone and body language suggest that he is unlikely to do so.

While he thinks he is simply expressing his own views on the project, he is sending out a message (whether deliberately or subconsciously) that these changes are not worthwhile.

This is disruptive to team and initiative unity.

5.2.3 Timing and frequency matter

As in any successful relationship, good timing is essential to getting things done.

Communication must be proportionate. It needs to be relevant and appropriate at the time it is made. For example, it is not sensible to send out information on good SLA performance during a major incident or to highlight minor changes during a major service launch.

We can make many clumsy mistakes, albeit innocently, when communicating as a service provider, including:

● Failing to appreciate and respond appropriately during key business periods when there is heightened activity and priority.

● Sending out updates about planned service downtime before it has been agreed with users.

● Issuing reports showing great performance statistics when there are major incidents or ongoing issues occurring.

● Sending out customer satisfaction surveys before incidents are closed, or sending surveys too often to the same people.

● Planning key project and change activities when there are higher-priority business activities taking place.

Image 5.1 Timing and frequency matter

- Over-communicating – that is, sending out too many messages or escalations, such that they lose their impact or are ignored.
- Submitting an ambitious business case when there are more pragmatic issues on the agenda that are likely to get a favourable response and budget approval.

We should consider two things in order to avoid these issues, as well as applying common sense, tact and diplomacy, of course:

- **Getting close to customers and stakeholders** Not everything can be defined regarding how we work together in terms of SLAs, operational level agreements (OLAs) and key performance indicators (KPIs). It is the relationships that count. Good relationships are based on developing intimacy, proximity and shared goals, all of which help to inform each party of what the other is doing, thinking, and about to do. This in turn helps to clarify when will be the best time to initiate contact and dialogue.
- **Understanding the bigger picture** We will be more likely to succeed if we are close to the people and teams that we need to communicate with and understand their perspective and priorities.

We can also be smart and use our networking and collaboration skills to choose the best and optimum moments to raise issues, requests, business cases etc. We should use feedback from, for example, surveys and global updates, to identify which approach works best, and which might be alienating our users.

5.2.3.1 ITSM considerations

- Planning and coordination of communications activity is essential, both within larger initiatives and within daily operations, to ensure that useful relationships are being developed and that the holistic view is always adopted.
- It is useful to coordinate the issuing of messages and initiative updates through a small team or an individual, who should ensure that messages are appropriate in content, context and timing.
- Updates on planned maintenance and downtime require liaison with relationship managers who are able to agree plans and highlight potential issues with the customer in order to manage what might be disruptive work.

- At a more strategic level, the business relationship manager (BRM) should be consulted with regard to timings and scheduling of projects, business cases etc., for advice on the most advantageous times for disruptive work.

- Carefully consider the scheduling of user escalation emails and customer satisfaction surveys. Although these are generally useful tools, when issued without consideration for the recipient, they can be seen to be intrusive and thoughtless.

- Less is more is a worthwhile maxim to follow. People will be more likely to read and comprehend updates if they are rare in frequency and short and simple in content.

5.2.4 There is no single method of communication

Everyone has different preferences and ways of sending and receiving communication (see Figure 5.3 for a selection of the various ways). It is advisable to utilize a number of different media and techniques to ensure that the intended audience is reached. This is highly understood in advertising, where marketers avail themselves of a variety of media to get their campaign messages out – for example, the marketing mix of newspaper, TV and billboard advertisements, plus publicity and promotion.

It helps to know who the audience is in order to select the most appropriate means of contact. It is not always possible with every individual but, where possible, appropriateness should be the prevailing guide: 'How can we best keep in touch with your team? What is the fastest way to get messages to you?'

It is beneficial to adhere to the two-way communication approach of checking that sent messages have been received, and whether the method of communication was appropriate. For example, if email was used but did not solicit the desired level of response, it might be time to try a different method of communication.

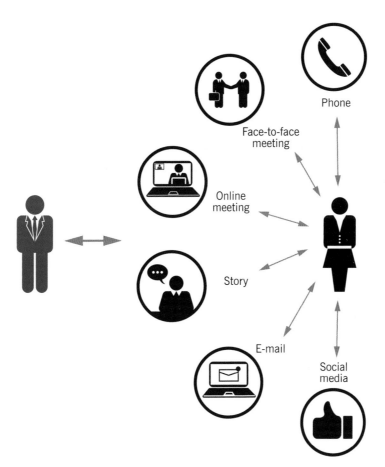

Figure 5.3 There is no single method of communication

It is useful to be aware of the different ways colleagues and customers work and what their individual communication styles are. Do they like small talk before getting down to business? (some do, some do not). Do they need lots of factual information? Are they more receptive to emotional or social kinds of conversations? People have preferred (and less preferred) ways of being contacted, whether that is face-to-face, phone, email, text etc. Tailoring the message to the recipient goes a long way towards prompting a positive response.

5.2.4.1 ITSM considerations

Try using the marketing mix of different forms of communication to reach a wider and more inclusive audience, beyond the traditional reporting and formal progress methods, including:

- Email
- Phone
- Conference calls/video-conferencing
- Social forums
- Personal contact
- Meetings
- Text and instant messaging
- Posters
- Postcards
- Webinars
- Screensavers
- Intranet pages
- Mouse mats.

It is essential when trying to influence or progress an issue – for example, a business case or long-term change – that alternative options are considered, for both the format and content of the message or document. Many business cases fail simply because they are poorly presented or through a lack of ability to make the case clearly and effectively. It is remarkable how often successful business cases were actually Plan B rather than Plan A.

Tip

Do not assume that every user wants to receive an automatic email update every time their incident is changed. They should be asked if that is appropriate.

5.2.5 The message is in the medium

The format and nature of a message can often determine the emotional response from the receiver. This will have a major impact on the level of importance, interest and understanding that will be given to it.

Care is needed in selecting the most appropriate format, style, size, frequency and medium for any given message. This will help to improve the chances of the message being read and understood, rather than simply ignored or deleted.

Ensure that each message and exchange of information helps to build a clear picture of the service and the relationship between parties, rather than detracting from it by focusing too closely on individual parts or issues.

> ### Example
> A company provides a very successful service in terms of availability and fulfilling their customers' needs. However, all the customer ever sees is notices about weekend downtime and incident management statistics. The customer develops an unbalanced and incorrect picture of the value the company delivers.

5.2.5.1 ITSM considerations

Considerations include:

- **Messages regarding service availability updates frequently get missed** To ensure a greater chance of being noticed, messages should be short and simple and use language that is easy to understand.

- **SLAs can stretch to hundreds of pages** The key content might simply be one table containing response and fix times. There may be circumstances where that one table is enough for the customer, rather than the full document, or where the table can be used as a summary at the front of the document, where it is more likely to be noticed.

- **System and process specifications for procurement are often large and detailed** Many of the processes and system functions contained in these specifications are universal. The documents should focus on the areas of differentiation, not on the generic.

- **Jargon, legalese and technical terms can be annoying** A non-technical, non-legal audience may feel alienated by the use of such terms. Keep them out of documentation and discussions as much as possible when communicating with these audiences.

- **Content, style and format must address the intended audience** Focus on delivering the intended message to the right people. For example, newspapers write and present the same information in completely different ways, depending on their target readership. Broadsheets use different language and images from tabloids. Using a similar approach can help to ensure that messages are delivered successfully.

5.3 COMMUNICATION TECHNIQUES

The act of communication can be broken down into four key areas:

- **Visual** Graphics, infographics, presentations etc.
- **Written** Documents, papers, email, digital etc.
- **Verbal** Face-to-face, telephone conversations etc.
- **Non-verbal** Face-to-face, body language, posture, clothing, components of phone calls such as tone of voice.

5.3.1 Fundamental steps in communication

These areas are the components of the basic steps that apply to all communication:

- **Introduction/preamble** Introductions and preambles are useful to set everyone at ease, while providing a defined frame around the business of the meeting. Small talk is useful as a low-risk means to get the conversation going, though the form may vary across cultures.

- **Information exchange** Each party has information they wish to obtain from the other. It is important to follow the two-way communication principle and ensure each person is heard. Non-verbal communication can help; the listener can indicate from nods and eye contact that they are following the speaker. This can be referred to as active listening.

- **Verbal handshake** The verbal handshake is an extension of active listening, where one or both parties play back their understanding of the content of the discussion, the next steps and action points, to show the message has been received and understood.

● **Closure** There is a skill in closing down a conversation that has run its course, where perhaps one party wants to continue with a social discussion or to go over the key points again. It is important to close off the conversation with a positive and forward-looking tone where possible, maybe with a summary of subsequent actions.

5.3.2 Communication planning

Communication activities should be planned like any other task. For large initiatives, they should be structured to focus on the key elements of the required communication. Planning can drive ownership and ensures the activity gets done.

A simple communication plan should answer the following:

● What message needs to be sent out and to whom?
● What is the purpose of the message?
● What is the best format and medium for each message?
● When does this need to be sent? By whom?
● What is the best way to test that the message has been understood?
● How can feedback be best encouraged, captured and acted upon?

Toolkit

More information about communication planning can be found in section 7.3, and a template for a stakeholder communication plan is provided in section 7.4.3.

5.3.3 Types of communication

5.3.3.1 Physical: face-to-face

Face-to-face is the best way to interact and build a relationship with someone.

Physical presence demands mutual respect and acknowledgement of the other person and their persona, interests, family background, etc. Through a reading of body language and other non-verbal means of communicating, face-to-face meetings give insight into the emotional engagement of the participants.

A direct conversation and discussion can cover a variety of points, at both a micro and macro level, and reach agreement relatively quickly, compared with the extended period an email exchange may take to reach a resolution.

5.3.3.2 Verbal

Like a physical conversation, telephone communication can be used to cut through issues and speed up the exchange of information. There are aspects of body language and emotional state that can be identified over the phone via non-verbal communication such as tone of voice, volume, language.

Telephone is a more suitable method of communication to resolve issues than email, where unnecessary misunderstandings can easily develop and escalate.

The development of immersive, ambient video-conferencing, as well as some simple collaboration tools, has increased the opportunity for what is essentially digital face-to-face interaction.

5.3.3.3 Email

Email is long-established as the predominant electronic means of communication for work. Though email is often criticized for its limitations, most organizations would struggle to function without it.

For short and simple messages, it has been replaced by short messaging systems (SMS) and instant messaging (IM), which are faster, simpler and cheaper. Email can be unsuitable for exchanges that involve conflict, or difficult or heated discussion, which might be better addressed in person or via telephone call.

Email is particularly useful for short, factual exchanges of information, particularly where written documentation is required. It can be used for confirmation of key points of a discussion, and as a means to contact a wide group of people simultaneously. By providing links, short notes and attachments, email can improve communication by giving both parties a record of administration and logistics information.

Some key email tips:

- Use email for short exchanges of information and reference.
- Tone of voice within an email can be misread, particularly when the email is too long and wordy. Keep emails short and to the point, polite, professional and positive.
- Avoid overusing whole words in capital letters, as it gives the impression that the author is shouting.
- It is important to balance formality and informality. Emails are not personal messages; they should not be too informal. Emails are not legal documents; they should not be overly formal.
- Make it clear where a response is required or an action is expected.
- Consider the impact on others of using CC and BCC – often, it is best to avoid unless absolutely necessary.
- If sending an email feels inappropriate, it may be preferable to pick up the phone.

5.3.3.4 Short messaging systems, instant messaging and social tools

SMS, IM and other social tools are simple and easy to use as a means to reach people quickly and directly, often without the formal shackles of email or even physical or telephone conversation.

It is important to consider using these tools only when appropriate and in an agreed or approved way. These messages can be open to misunderstanding and misinterpretation, especially if they make excessive use of text-speak. It is better to use this method when the recipient is known to understand the lexicon of texting. Many organizations have policies that govern the use of SMS, IM etc.

5.3.3.5 Graphics

Pictures, charts, cartoons and colourful images are an excellent way to get a message across. Pictorial images engage more with the emotions and tend to be better remembered. This is a reminder that, when communicating, always seek the easiest and fastest means for the recipient to receive an idea.

Reporting makes great use of graphics. For example, an appropriate use of colour in a chart or graph can be a great way to highlight variance. Real-time dashboards are similarly an excellent way to present information about service progress and quality, particularly in operational areas such as service desks.

'Infographics' is a term used to describe how to communicate information and ideas, and to relate actions and analysis, using graphical summary forms rather than text-based documents.

5.3.3.6 Storytelling

Storytelling is a long-established method of communicating information and ideas which of late has found a new appreciation in the work environment as a highly effective tool.

In order to process and understand a story, the recipient needs to effectively recreate it in their own mind, using the imagery the storyteller conveys. The process of stimulating the imagination improves the chance that the content will be retained in memory. The imagination also uses more parts of the brain in comparison with passively reading data, leading to a significantly better retention rate than would be the case with text, bullet lists or other forms of dry data. Storytelling is used widely in presentations and training classes.

Some organizations use the principles of good storytelling as a means to enhance the way their communication is delivered. This may be by mandating the use of a single page and/or graphical format – for example, the business model canvas – for proposals, business cases and presentations.

Storytelling utilizes key elements of communication, makes use of varied and appropriate imagery and imagination to engage and involve participants, and uses feedback, including body language and other forms of non-verbal communication, from participants to check that the message has been understood. Ultimately, storytelling is the most intrinsic and human of communication techniques, which can be used for information exchange and influence.

Storytelling is not for everyone, but it is a strong portfolio tool to have when trying to win people over to a new process or way of working. Not everyone using this technique needs to be an expert storyteller, although, in many situations, a powerful anecdote or analogy can provide more clarity than a long slide deck.

5.3.3.7 Reports

Reporting is an excellent medium for communication. It can be used effectively to identify and highlight issues, particularly across teams and departments, which otherwise may not be obvious.

For example:

● Transparency in identifying agent logging and resolution performance in a service desk

● Highlighting areas where resolver groups are not meeting SLAs or OLAs

● Clarifying that the IT organization is delivering as promised

● Identifying areas where service availability needs to be improved.

As described in section 5.3.3.5, graphics are a vital element in successful reporting and the presentation of information. While the presentation itself is important, it is essential that the information and metrics being presented are relevant to the audience.

See Chapter 4 for details on assessment criteria and example KPIs.

5.3.3.8 Effective meetings and workshops

Meetings and workshops are essential tools for achieving progress within organizations. All good communicators who run initiatives know how to run meetings and workshops effectively. They should support the aims and practical goals of the project and act as an accelerated point of information exchange, decision-making and agreement to action.

Some key points:

● Meetings must be run to meet the organization's or initiative's goals. They should be timely and follow a set agenda, with action minutes quickly distributed after the meeting. They are not intended as forums for chat.

● Meetings need to have a clear agenda and purpose – for example, to distribute and explain new service details and achieve agreement on how new processes should be followed, to decide on whether to bid for a tender, or to resolve a conflict around misuse of a process.

● The quality and delivery of a meeting can be a useful gauge of the culture of the organization, demonstrating professionalism and competence if run on time, or poor culture if they are not taken seriously.

● Workshops are a great way to move a project forward by getting key people together to share experience and build agreement, common understanding and momentum.

● The quality of delivery of the workshop or meeting can determine the success of the wider initiative or service as a whole. For example, a workshop can be used to carry out basic learning and gain consensus, to get issues out into the open within a peer group, to brainstorm new ideas or changes to services and ways of working.

● Workshops and meetings serve as communal direct communication, complete with human contact and the opportunity for speedy face-to-face issue resolution and decision-making. There is real value in having a group of people together in the same room for a period of time, focused on an issue and moving as one to an agreed solution.

Toolkit

The workshop and meeting action plan can be found in section 7.3.2.

The meeting notes template can be found in section 7.3.3.

5.3.3.9 Communicate by example

One of the most effective means of communicating and expressing a view or position is by showing other people how to do it. This can extend to many aspects of a person's character and communication style, such as how they talk on the phone, how they dress and physically carry themselves, how they address people to show respect and courtesy. Communicating by example is a potent way to express a view – walking the walk, as it were, not simply talking the talk.

Service desks have long used the technique of bringing in experienced external analysts who can demonstrate how to talk to customers and manage issues.

For managers, communicating by example is a vital part of their skill portfolio. No manager can expect to lead effectively if they do not demonstrate the performance and capability traits they expect from their staff. Managers need to do as they say and act consistently in order to gain respect.

It can be difficult to train or explain to staff that they are expected to be open, to come up with new ideas, to be proactive, etc. This expectation may be best communicated by their leaders and managers showing the same openness and willingness to fail.

5.3.3.10 Record logging quality and categorization

The electronic forms that IT and service provider staff fill out to record incidents, problems, changes etc., often within an ITSM tool, are an important means of communication within ITSM. Service desk and support analyst staff use these forms every day, and by filling out the form with the correct level of detail, they can improve the effectiveness of the process for their customers, as well as generating valuable data for reporting, problem management and continual service improvement.

The quality and effectiveness of the classification and categorization of the audit trail information (that is logged and updated within these forms) are of great value to the organization. It is important to:

- define clear and effective categories and values for fields and tables
- ensure that all staff are aware of what is expected of them in terms of data quality. For example, simply logging 'done' or 'fixed' is of no value
- produce high-quality information that can be reused in the future to reduce investigation time.

Often these points are ignored and the investment made in ITSM systems is not realized. The proper and effective use of these tools is an essential means of communicating information.

5.3.3.11 Training and education

Training is a central form of communication. It is a direct means of giving people knowledge, skills and information, as well as providing a place to test and develop the confidence to use these skills in the workplace.

Training can be used to show people that they are valued, and it is an opportunity to exchange ideas and new skills, and to discuss how to effect improvement in the workplace.

Simulations and immersive and experiential learning – games, role playing etc. – are effective means of communicating ideas without making the training too formal. They are great ways to embed ideas as experiences that happen on these courses tend to be remembered long after memories of slides with bullet points have faded away.

Many vocations use simulation or testing environments to improve the skills and capabilities of their people. For example, pilots use flight simulators, and firefighters and emergency services run exercises to simulate accidents and disasters. Simulations and testing environments provide learning platforms that are safe and where trainees can experiment, secure in the knowledge that mistakes will not result in disaster.

Simulations, including ITIL and ITSM simulations, mimic real-life situations and are a powerful way to convey key messages about the need for planning, collaboration and good communication. They can also be used to ensure that access is provided to processes and activities that might happen rarely in the real work environment, but which still need to be planned for and tested.

Experiential learning is useful for the same physiological reasons that storytelling works. That is, emotional engagement combined with creative brain activity results in lessons learned and knowledge gained becoming embedded and memorable.

See section 6.6.4 for more information regarding communication around change.

5.3.3.12 Business case

Business cases are a very specific form of communication, designed to achieve a particular outcome, e.g. a commitment to funding or business decision and approval.

It is important to understand that business cases are regarded as catalysts – that is, they are seen as part of a process of interaction and communication that moves a decision forward. In that sense, the goal of the business case is to meet the requirements of the recipient as much as possible, in terms of their goals, an understanding of the issues affecting them, and of the time available to deal with the outcome of the decision.

The key principles of communication should be utilized. The recipient should be identified in order to work towards their preferred style of presentation, minimizing extraneous content and ensuring that the timing and format are appropriate for them.

If the first iteration fails, it is worth considering other approaches. Many failed business cases are approved at the second or third attempt, simply because the timing, format and message have been honed until they are relevant to the recipient.

Tools such as the business model canvas can be useful as an interactive and collaborative means to develop the ideas and necessary components of the business case. The business model canvas features a chart where key elements can be defined, such as key activities, key resources, value propositions, customers, channels, finance and revenue streams. Participants can collaboratively add or remove content in the process of preparing it for presentation to the relevant decision-makers.

Toolkit

For more information on business cases, including a business case worksheet, see section 7.3.4.

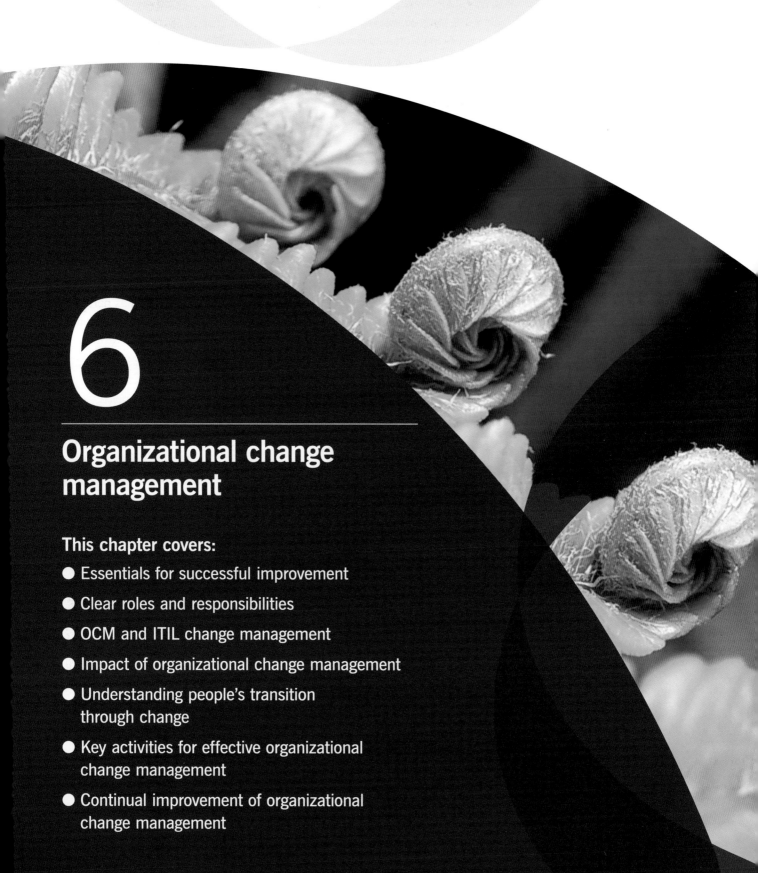

6

Organizational change management

This chapter covers:

- Essentials for successful improvement
- Clear roles and responsibilities
- OCM and ITIL change management
- Impact of organizational change management
- Understanding people's transition through change
- Key activities for effective organizational change management
- Continual improvement of organizational change management

6 Organizational change management

Organizational change management (OCM) is concerned with the people side of change. It is a structured approach that ensures improvements are implemented smoothly and successfully for lasting benefit.

Improvements invariably require people to change the way they work, to change behaviour and sometimes to change role. Whatever is being changed in relation to IT service management (ITSM) process improvement, technology change, new service introduction, service improvement etc., it involves people. Regardless of the scope, size or nature of the improvement initiative, there will be an impact on people. It may not be a huge impact but some change in people's behaviour will be required.

When people understand the purpose of the change, how it will affect them and their job, and when they believe in the importance and benefits of the change, then improvement initiatives are far more likely to succeed.

The aim of OCM is to win the hearts and minds of each individual affected by the change in order to reduce or remove resistance and ensure the change is implemented and sustained successfully. In the process, individuals, teams and organizations are transitioned from their current state to a desired future state where the change has been made and is working as planned.

OCM applies to both IT and non-IT changes, of all manners, shapes and sizes. Even initiatives not run as formal projects due to their size and nature will require OCM capabilities.

Accountability for OCM cannot be transferred to an external supplier. Someone within the organization itself is accountable for OCM, even if responsibility for the execution of OCM activities is delegated.

Key message

Whether the improvement is being driven via change management, project management, programme management or any other approach, OCM is not to be seen as an additional framework. It is an integral part of each of those approaches and it underpins every improvement initiative.

Definition: Capability

A capability is the ability of an organization or person or process to carry out an activity.

Definition: Function

A function is an organizational entity – for example, a team or group of people, typically characterized by a special area of knowledge and/or experience.

Key message

OCM is a capability and critical competency. It is not necessarily a function within an organization.

Some organizations have a dedicated OCM function or team but this guidance will consider OCM a capability, as it is a set of deliberate and conscious actions that take place while making ITSM improvements.

6.1 ESSENTIALS FOR SUCCESSFUL IMPROVEMENT

For successful improvement, OCM needs to ensure that the following are present:

- **Clear and relevant objectives** In order to gain maximum support, an improvement will require clear and relevant objectives which make sense in the context of the organization into which the improvement is being introduced. These objectives should be regularly communicated and should be based on what the customer determines is of value, not what the service provider believes is of value.

- **Strong and committed leadership** It is critical that the improvement has the active support of sponsors and day-to-day leaders within the organization. A sponsor is a manager or business leader required to advocate for, and who can authorize, the change. Each leader should be identified and their roles and responsibilities clearly communicated to the stakeholders of the improvement initiative, which can be managed through the creation of a sponsor roadmap.

- **Willing participants** The improvement needs participants who are willing to make the required change. Not everyone will be on board with the change and may resist it for a variety of reasons. OCM allows for the resistance to be brought to the fore and overcome using a resistance management plan.

- **Prepared participants** The improvement may require changes in people's working practices and/or the tools they use to do their jobs. People are more willing to change if they feel they are suitably prepared. OCM uses a training plan to ensure that the impacted people have the right skills and knowledge to successfully make the change, and a communication plan to manage how participants are updated about the change.

Toolkit

A training plan template can be found in section 7.4.10. A stakeholder communication plan template can be found in section 7.4.3.

- **Sustained improvement** Many improvements fail because, after a while, people revert to old ways of working. OCM seeks to continually reinforce the value of the change through regular communication and the support of sponsors and leaders.

Key message

It is important to note that OCM is entirely scalable. Whether the improvement impacts one person, 10 people, 100 people or more, it still changes the way in which each person is required to work or behave.

It is important to ensure that each person is moved from the current state to the desired state, and that the improvement is sustained. This will require effective communication, and possibly stakeholder management, sponsorship, empowerment, resistance management and continual positive reinforcement. At a minimum, each person needs to understand the need for the planned change.

Consideration should always be given to the potential impact any improvement initiative has on others.

6.2 CLEAR ROLES AND RESPONSIBILITIES

For stakeholders and sponsors, it is imperative that clear roles and responsibilities are defined for each person and/or role, including those involved in driving the ITSM improvement initiative.

A RACI model authority matrix, as shown in Table 6.1, is a useful tool for identifying the level of participation of various roles in the delivery of tasks, deliverables, or activities within a given process – for example, within incident management.

A RACI model has four participation types:

● **Responsible** The roles that directly work on the task. There must be at least one role with a participation type of 'responsible', though others can be delegated to assist in the work as required

● **Accountable** The role ultimately answerable for the correct and thorough completion of the activity, deliverable or task. This person delegates the work to those responsible. There must be only one 'accountable' specified for a particular task or deliverable

● **Consulted** The roles whose opinions are sought and with whom there is two-way communication

● **Informed** The roles that are kept up-to-date on progress, requiring just one-way communication.

Definition: Role

A set of responsibilities, activities and authorities assigned to a person or team. A role is defined in a process or function. One person or team may have multiple roles – for example, the roles of configuration manager and change manager may be carried out by a single person. 'Role' is also used to describe the purpose of something or what it is used for.

A role is an associated set of tasks. They may be performed by more than one person – for example, many people may perform the role of reinforcing sponsor. One individual may perform many roles – for example, an individual may simultaneously be a reinforcing sponsor, a project manager and/or a **service owner**.

The RACI model is constructed with a vertical axis (left-hand column) containing a list of activities, tasks or deliverables that need to be completed. The horizontal axis (top row) contains the roles that will participate in a responsible, accountable, consulted or informed manner.

Table 6.1 RACI matrix example

Activity	Role 1	Role 2	Role 3	Role 4
Activity 1	A/R	R	C	I
Activity 2	R	A/R	C	I
Activity 3	R	A	I	C

Example

An IT department needs to transition a remote service desk into the corporate service desk tool.

Overall accountability for the transition rests with the corporate service desk manager. Responsibility for the remote service desk rests with the remote HR manager.

A high-level RACI model for this transition can be seen in Table 6.2.

Table 6.2 An example of a RACI model

	Corporate service desk manager	Remote service desk analyst	Remote HR manager	Corporate IT manager	Corporate service desk analyst
Launch	A/R	I	R	C	I
Commence transition	A/R	C	R	C	C
Go-live	A/R	C	R	C	C
Post go-live review	A/R	C	C	C	C

Toolkit

A template of a RACI model authority matrix can be found in section 7.4.6.

6.3 OCM AND ITIL CHANGE MANAGEMENT

Definition: Organizational change management

An approach for managing the effect of change on people, which could be because of new business processes, changes in organizational structure or cultural changes within an enterprise. Simply put, OCM addresses the people side of change management.

OCM helps people to think, and feel, differently about changes, regardless of the scale of the change, as it provides a better understanding of how they and their role are impacted.

Definition: Change management

The process responsible for coordinating the lifecycle of all changes. The process is triggered by a request for change (RFC) or change proposal. The primary objective of change management is to enable beneficial changes to be made with minimum disruption to IT services – that is, they are registered, evaluated, prioritized, planned, tested, implemented and documented.

Significant improvements are likely to be initiated through the CSI approach rather than specifically by raising an RFC and will usually be run as projects or programmes with defined objectives.

6.4 IMPACT OF ORGANIZATIONAL CHANGE MANAGEMENT

6.4.1 OCM and ITSM improvement initiatives

Regardless of the size, scope and nature of an ITSM improvement initiative, its success is contingent on how OCM is approached. Resistance to change is normal; people become comfortable with the status quo. OCM is important in that it ensures everyone understands the need for change and, where resistance is encountered, manages it effectively.

In adopting an ITSM approach to service provision, one or more of the following sources of resistance are likely to be encountered:

● No management commitment
● People saying yes, but meaning no

● People going back to old ways of working
● Process managers acting without the requisite authority
● Lack of visible sponsorship and support
● No continual improvement focus (lack of sustained momentum)
● Inability to establish a sense of urgency and a compelling need for change
● Improvements made without adequate engagement and communication
● Inability to demonstrate enough value to the business to elicit support
● Everything being of equally high priority.

Toolkit

Section 7.4 contains two assessments that can be used to determine the OCM effort and resources required for your ITSM improvement initiative.

6.4.2 OCM and project management

All projects require a deliberate OCM component to be successful.

Prosci, a world leader in organizational change management benchmarking research, reports that projects with excellent OCM effectiveness are six times more likely to meet or exceed project objectives.

A McKinsey study (LaClair and Rao, 2002) investigated projects in more than 40 organizations. The study examined many variables and, in particular, the effect of an OCM programme on a project's **return on investment (ROI)**. The study showed that ROI was 143% when a strong OCM programme was included as part of the initiative and only 35% when there was a weak OCM programme.

Toolkit

Section 7.4.14 contains a list of OCM frameworks and methodologies.

6.5 UNDERSTANDING PEOPLE'S TRANSITION THROUGH CHANGE

Some people see change as a positive exercise that will bring an enhanced future. However, regardless of how much thought has gone into an improvement initiative, some people within any organization are likely to be wary of change. Understanding how they feel will guide the communication plan and resistance management activities.

6.5.1 Emotional responses to change

Reaction to change is likely to be emotional rather than rational.

It is unlikely that the emotional response will be uniform across the organization. People respond in different ways. For some, change may be seen as positive. Others may see it as having an adverse impact, either on them personally or on the organization as a whole.

Key message

It is important to realize that, however clear it is to you that the improvement initiative makes sense and that the benefits are obvious, this may not be the case for others.

Every person is different, with different values and beliefs. They may see the improvement from a different perspective. It is important to recognize the stages people go through during times of change so that those struggling to make the change can be assisted through the process.

6.5.2 The change curve

The change curve is a widely used model for understanding how people respond to change. There are many variations, but they are generally based on the Kübler-Ross model commonly known as the grief cycle (Kübler-Ross, 1969).

Her five-stage theory sought to explain how people deal with catastrophic personal loss such as death or being diagnosed with a terminal illness. It was later recognized that this theory also applied to how people respond to change. According to Kübler-Ross, people react to change according to a specific pattern. There are two dimensions involved: time and emotional response. Over time, the emotional response changes and the available energy fluctuates.

There are five stages: denial, anger, bargaining, depression and acceptance.

The change curve depicted in Figure 6.1 shows the five stages that Kübler-Ross describes, along with several extensions. The figure notes the responses that can be given to individuals who are in each stage of the curve. The curve not only illustrates the different states and stages an individual may go through in response to an improvement initiative, but also the complexity of transitioning a person from the current state to the desired state. It makes it very clear why OCM is so important.

Just because a handful of people are at the acceptance stage does not mean the improvement initiative is complete. Individuals may be at different stages of the change curve at any one time. It is important to recognize where each person is on the curve and to work to bring each of them to acceptance. It is also important to recognize that people can move up and down the change curve. It is not a one-way process.

It is only by helping everyone to accept the change that, with continuing reinforcement, the improvement has a chance to become embedded. Without reinforcement, people tend to revert to old ways of working and the improvement becomes undone.

6.5.2.1 Denial

People in the denial stage may say:

> 'There is no need to change – the way we do things now is just fine.'

> 'It is just another fad and it simply won't happen.'

This is the stage where the reality of the change is first felt. The result is denial. A person undergoing denial might ignore the fact that the change has been announced and carry on as if nothing has happened.

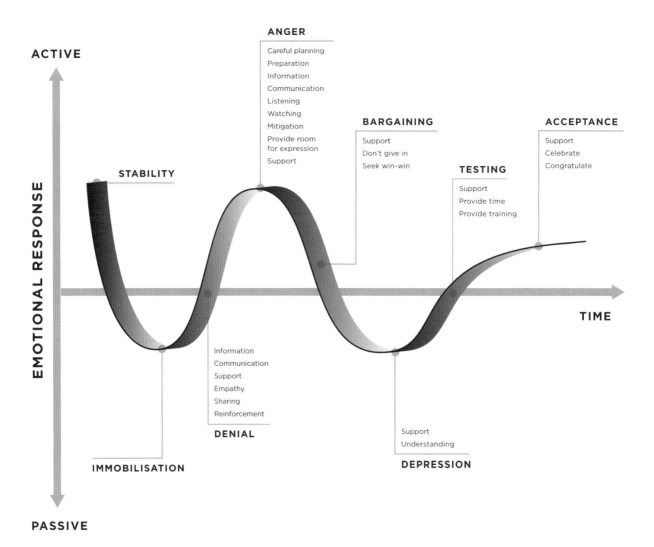

Figure 6.1 The change curve

Good information and communication are essential at this stage. Regular communication regarding the change, the reason for the change and where employees and colleagues can go to get more information are helpful at this stage. Make sure the communication channels are open but do not overwhelm people with vast amounts of information all at once. Provide information in a piecemeal fashion while ensuring they are aware they can obtain more information as and when they need it.

Strong leadership support for the change is vital, with the right messages conveyed to create a sense of urgency and to reinforce the need for the change.

People can be moved from denial into anger through empathy. Allow them to share their fears and resentment while reinforcing the message that the change is going to happen.

6.5.2.2 Anger

People in the anger stage may say:

> 'Why me? It's not fair! Who is to blame? Why not you? It'll never work. I'm not doing that.'

This is the stage of the most emotional outpouring. People will look for someone to blame and express anger at those they perceive not to be impacted by the change. Careful management is needed to avoid crisis or chaos.

It is paramount to plan carefully for this stage. Consider what impact the change will have on individuals and what objections they may raise. Reflect these considerations in the communication and information being provided so that objections can be mitigated as early as possible. Of course, there will be responses that cannot be foreseen. It is important to listen to what is being said and watch what is happening so that mitigating action can take place in a timely manner.

It is also important to allow those affected to express their anger as long as it does not become destructive. Provide support and opportunities for them to air their grievances. Lack of response at this stage can result in a move back into the denial stage.

6.5.2.3 Bargaining

People in the bargaining stage may say:

'I'll do a different job. Can you wait till it is more convenient for me?'

This is the stage where there is recognition that the change will happen so bargaining activities come into play to try to postpone or delay the change and its impact on the individual.

Bargaining could include staff seeking an alternative position within the organization that they perceive will not be impacted by the change, or trying to negotiate a partial adoption of the change. Employees will talk about their tenure, loyalty, performance records etc. to support their bargaining.

The key here is to provide support and not agree to anything that cannot be provided. If there are opportunities for a win-win situation where something can be offered in exchange for support of the change, that should be explored.

6.5.2.4 Depression

People in the depression stage may say:

'What's the point? Why bother?'

This is the stage that the certainty of the change is realized and reluctant acceptance results.

Depression sets in and those affected turn in towards themselves, refusing any help or support from others. Everything seems bleak and desolate. During this stage, there may be a rise in absenteeism, sick leave, poor performance, poor punctuality etc.

The best response at this stage is support and understanding, including providing access to counselling services either via HR or unions, and to people who have been through the process. It is important that employees and colleagues do not feel alone and know that support is readily available and forthcoming.

6.5.2.5 Testing

People in the testing stage may say:

'OK, maybe I'll listen. What's in it for me?'

This is the stage where there is a move out of depression as the realization that the change is going to happen occurs. Those affected now explore change and try new options to see if they can make the new way work for them. This is a period of exploration and learning, a turning point for both the individual and the organization.

Give support to explore and test what the change means. Ensure that enough time is provided to allow this to happen fully. Provide training so that they are well prepared for the change. Build in time to the day-to-day activities to allow for learning and exploration. Do not expect this to happen as an addition to business as usual.

6.5.2.6 Acceptance

People in the acceptance stage will say:

'It's going to be OK.'

This is the stage where the individual accepts that the change is going to happen and finds a way to move forward. They take responsibility for their actions. Acceptance may be initially a resistant acceptance but it should become a positive acceptance over time.

Continue offering support to those who were impacted by the change who may have found themselves in new roles or have had to develop their role within the organization. The key is to celebrate success. Celebrate the successful implementation of the change as an organization and congratulate individuals on getting through the change process. Involve everyone as this celebration of success will smooth the implementation of the next change.

6.5.3 William Bridges' three phases of transition

An alternative but similar approach to the change curve is a model William Bridges described in his book, *Managing Transitions* (Bridges, 2003). According to Bridges' theory, change is situational. Transition, on the other hand, is a psychological, three-phase process that people go through as they internalize and come to terms with the details of the new situation brought about by the change.

The process, as shown in Figure 6.2, consists of the following three phases:

● Ending, losing and letting go
● The neutral zone
● The new beginning.

6.5.3.1 Ending, losing, letting go

The process of letting go of the past can bring up feelings of sadness, grief and loss, as well as relief or anticipation of a possible new future. The starting point for dealing with change is not the outcome, but the ending the person must make to leave the old way behind.

Bridges identifies five aspects of the natural ending experience: disengagement, dismantling, dis-identification, disenchantment and disorientation.

In the ending, losing, letting go phase, people express anger, bargaining, anxiety, sadness, disorientation and depression, among other emotions.

Key message
● Treat the past with respect
● Help compensate for losses
● Give people the right information
● Be empathetic
● Sympathize
● Make the endings
● Help define what is over and what is not.

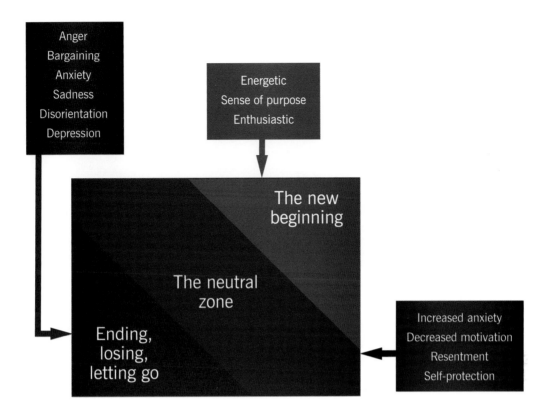

Figure 6.2 William Bridges' three phases of transition

6.5.3.2 The neutral zone

The neutral zone is that in-between place where people lose the sense of relatedness and purpose due to a person's identity being tied up in the old way of working. At this stage, there are no new anchors to give context or meaning, which can cause confusion and pain.

The neutral zone is a place of both risk and opportunity. It is risky because people are unsure of the process being created and may become anxious, which may cause productivity to fall. Old weaknesses, compensated for in the old way of working, may rise to the surface – for example, if customer service has always been weak, it gets worse in the neutral zone. People may get mixed signals between the old regime and the new, and they may get polarized one way or the other, leading to tension and discord. In addition, until the new regime becomes embedded, the new arrangements are vulnerable to internal or external shocks.

For these reasons, transitions through the neutral zone need to be carefully managed.

In the neutral zone, people demonstrate anxiety, lack of motivation, disorientation, resentfulness and self-protection, among other emotions.

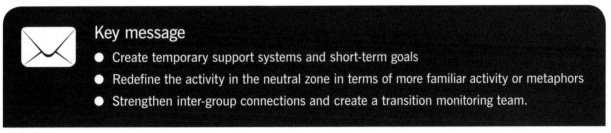

Key message
- Create temporary support systems and short-term goals
- Redefine the activity in the neutral zone in terms of more familiar activity or metaphors
- Strengthen inter-group connections and create a transition monitoring team.

Note that, despite the uncertainty it generates, the neutral zone is also a place of creative opportunity. As people and systems unfreeze from the old systems and have not yet frozen into the new systems, there is opportunity to identify and realize change, and find new ways of doing things.

6.5.3.3 The new beginning

The new beginning phase involves assisting people to develop the new identity, experience the new energy, and discover the new sense of purpose that make the change begin to work.

Bridges distinguishes between starts and beginnings. A start occurs when people start doing new things and start enacting the changes. A beginning occurs, however, only when the personal, psychological and behavioural change takes place and people take on new behaviours and identities.

Key message

During the new beginning phase, define a clear path for the future by clarifying and communicating the purpose of the transition, painting a picture of what the future looks like, and laying out a step-by-step plan for phasing in the change and for the part each person will play in both the plan and the outcome.

These tactics will help people shape new identities to replace the old identities they gave up when they let go of the old way of working. But if the change is to be retained, there needs to be reinforcement.

Key message

● Create consistent messaging
● Identify quick wins
● Symbolize the new identity
● Celebrate success.

When people transition into the new-beginning phase, they will have more energy, a new sense of purpose and enthusiasm.

6.5.4 Gartner hype cycle

The Gartner hype cycle is a graphical representation of the lifecycle stages that a technology, application or concept goes through from conception through to maturity and widespread adoption, and how people react as it matures.

Businesses use the hype cycle to guide decisions in accordance with their level of comfort with risk. Each stage of the cycle is associated with its own risks and opportunities. The hype cycle's stages are often used as reference points in marketing and technology reporting:

● **Technology trigger** A potential technology breakthrough begins the cycle. Early proof-of-concept stories and media interest trigger significant publicity. Often no usable products exist and commercial viability is unproven.

● **Peak of inflated expectations** Early publicity produces a number of success stories. These are often accompanied by reports of failures. Some organizations take action to adopt; the majority do not.

● **Trough of disillusionment** Interest wanes as experiments and implementations fail to deliver. Producers of the technology regroup or fail. Investments continue only if the surviving providers improve their products to the satisfaction of early adopters.

● **Slope of enlightenment** Instances of how the technology can benefit the enterprise become apparent and more widely understood. Second- and third-generation products appear from technology providers. More enterprises fund **pilots**; conservative companies remain cautious.

● **Plateau of productivity** Mainstream adoption occurs. Criteria for assessing provider viability are more clearly defined. The technology's broad market applicability and relevance pay off.

The hype cycle illustrates that, with ITSM initiatives, expectations may be inflated; without effective OCM, a trough of disillusionment may result.

Key message

Make sure the improvement sets clearly defined scope, goals and objectives, and makes it clear when the benefits will occur and what change the improvement is not intended to realize.

Often with ITSM improvement initiatives, the expectations are high and assumptions made about what will be delivered and when. If results are perceived to have not been achieved, people can become disillusioned with ITSM. The slope of enlightenment can be reached by implementing and communicating quick wins to demonstrate the benefits of ITSM.

Toolkit

Section 7.4 contains additional references to material covering transition through change.

6.6 KEY ACTIVITIES FOR EFFECTIVE ORGANIZATIONAL CHANGE MANAGEMENT

The key activities shown in Table 6.3, which build on John Kotter's eight steps in *Leading Change* (Kotter, 1996), represent a distillation of the best practice with regards OCM approaches and experiences.

Depending on the size and nature of the improvement initiative, some activities may not be relevant. However, all improvement initiatives need a degree of OCM. At a minimum, an improvement initiative needs effective communication.

Table 6.3 Key activities for effective OCM

Activity	Helps to deliver
Create a sense of urgency	Clear and relevant objectives; willing participants
Stakeholder management	Strong and committed leadership
Sponsor management	Strong and committed leadership
Communication	Prepared participants; willing participants
Empowerment	Prepared participants
Resistance management	Willing participants
Reinforcement	Sustained improvement

Toolkit

Section 7.4 contains two assessments to aid in understanding the degree of organizational change your initiative will need.

Tip

When embarking on OCM activities to support your improvement initiative, do not forget to look into the resources already established within your organization. There may be a team of people carrying out OCM activities whose skills and experience can be leveraged.

Introduce your initiative with good communication and perhaps training. It is important you understand what activities you want help with and why the activities need to be done.

HR is a good place to start your research within the company.

6.6.1 Create a sense of urgency

Creating a sense of urgency alerts the organization to the impending change and begins the preparation for change. Leaders must position the change as an opportunity that appeals to individuals' heads and hearts, with the goal of raising a large, urgent crowd of volunteers. A sense of urgency is created by:

● Selling the value of a future state

● Making the status quo a dangerous place for people to remain.

There needs to be a compelling narrative which explains why it is not in people's best interest for the organization to stay in its current state. These could include:

● **Bringing the outside in** A we-know-best culture reduces urgency. When people do not see external opportunities or hazards, complacency grows

● **Sharing bad news with the organization**

● **Requiring managers and employees to talk regularly** Talking to unhappy suppliers, customers and other stakeholders helps them to understand any concerns directly

● **Sharing data** Information that supports the claim that change is necessary should be shared throughout the organization

● **Aligning actions with communications** Ensuring organizational decisions and management actions are in agreement with change communications.

Communication is critical. It is important that the message is clear and honest, and that it creates a sense of urgency rather than doom. By creating both a compelling picture of a desired future and the danger of accepting the status quo, the chances of gaining people's commitment to the change effort is greatly increased.

Key message

There is a difference between leadership and management:

● Leadership provides direction, encouragement and inspiration to make change happen

● Management is primarily an organizational role, coordinating people's efforts and allocating resources to maximize efficiency in achieving identified goals.

Frequently, managers do not understand the behaviour required to lead change. Clear roles and responsibilities for everyone involved in an improvement initiative throughout its duration are essential for the success of the improvement (see section 6.2 on roles and responsibilities).

6.6.2 Stakeholder management

Stakeholder management is an important discipline used to win the support of others. Stakeholders include anyone who has a vested interest in the improvement initiative, from staff participants to suppliers, business partners, managers, partners, leaders and sponsors. It is critical to identify the people needed to support the change and determine the communication needed to win and keep their support.

The benefits of stakeholder management are:

● The opinions of the most powerful stakeholders can be used to shape the initiative at an early stage. Not only does this make it more likely that they will demonstrate support, but their input can also improve the quality of the initiative.

● Gaining support from powerful stakeholders can help win more resources, which makes it more likely that the initiative will be successful.

● By communicating with stakeholders early and frequently, they will understand the nature and benefits of the initiative, which will ensure their vocal support.

● Reaction to the initiative can be anticipated and actions that will win support can be built into the plan.

Note that stakeholders include people outside the organization such as suppliers, partners and shareholders.

6.6.2.1 Stakeholder analysis

Stakeholder analysis is a means to identify and characterize each of the individuals or teams who have a vested interest in the improvement initiative.

Step 1 – Identify the stakeholders

The first step is to identify your stakeholders. Consider the people who are impacted by the improvement initiative, who have influence or power over it, or have an interest in its successful or unsuccessful conclusion.

These may include:

● Managers
● Senior executives
● Employees
● Shareholders
● Customers
● Users
● Suppliers
● Community
● Partners
● Regulators.

Map the stakeholder information onto a stakeholder analysis worksheet.

Note that although stakeholders may be groups, organizations or individuals, ultimately the communication is with people. Make sure to identify the correct individual stakeholders within a stakeholder organization or group.

Toolkit
A stakeholder analysis worksheet can be found in section 7.4.1.

The following information should be captured in the worksheet:

● **Stakeholders** The groups or individuals impacted or who have an interest in the improvement initiative

● **Impact** The impact of the improvement initiative on the stakeholder group or individual

● **Expectations** The goal of the initiative from the stakeholder's point of view.

Toolkit

The sponsor diagram and the sponsor roadmap described in sections 7.4.4 and 7.4.5 can help map the sponsors and their relationships to the organization.

Step 2 – Prioritize stakeholders

Once the stakeholders have been identified and characterized, the next step is to work out the power, influence and interest of each stakeholder. The goal is to develop an understanding of the most important stakeholders in order to know how they are likely to respond and how their support can be won. This analysis can be recorded on a stakeholder map charting power and interest, as shown in Figure 6.3.

Stakeholders can be divided into four categories: major, critical, significant and minor. An individual's position on the grid shows their value to the initiative:

● **Critical stakeholders** Must be fully engaged with the initiative and satisfied with the improvement

● **Major stakeholders** Must be satisfied with the improvement but not so involved in driving the initiative

● **Significant stakeholders** Should be kept adequately informed and engaged in order to ensure the initiative causes no major issues

● **Minor stakeholders** Need monitoring and informing but communication should be kept to a minimum.

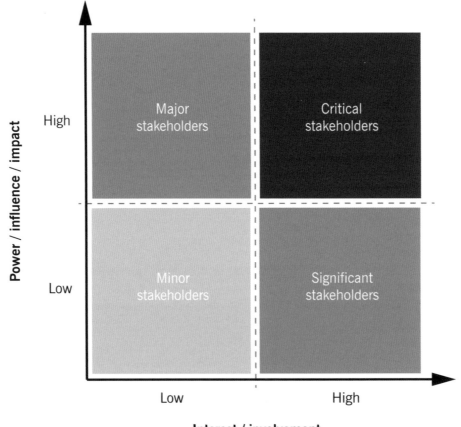

Figure 6.3 Stakeholder map (power/interest grid)

Toolkit

An example of a stakeholder map recording the most important stakeholders is given in Figure 7.4 (section 7.4.2).

Step 3 – Understanding key stakeholders

It is important to understand how the key stakeholders are likely to feel about and react to the improvement initiative, how they can best be engaged and what form of communication works best for them.

● What interest do they have in the outcome of the work? Is it positive or negative?
● What is their primary motivation?
● What information do they need?
● How do they want to receive information? What is the best way to communicate with them?
● What is their current opinion of the initiative? Is it based on good information?
● Who influences their opinions? Are some of these influencers important stakeholders in their own right?
● If they are unlikely to be positive, what will win them around to support the improvement?
● If it is doubtful they can be won over, how can their opposition be managed?
● Who might be influenced by their opinions? Are they stakeholders in their own right?

Tip

Talk to the stakeholders directly – people are often open about their views, and asking their opinions can be a first step in building a successful relationship with them.

The stakeholder map will show which stakeholders could be advocates and supporters of the improvement initiative, and which may be opponents or critics. Colour-coding can assist here: show advocates and supporters in green, opponents and critics in red, and neutrals in orange.

Toolkit

An example of a stakeholder map with colour-coded stakeholders is included in section 7.4.2 (Figure 7.4).

6.6.2.2 Stakeholder planning

Once the stakeholders are mapped out, the next step is to plan the best way of communicating with each stakeholder, which will be guided by their position on the grid.

Plan the approach

The amount of time to be allocated to managing stakeholders depends on the size and difficulty of the improvement initiative, the time available for communication, and the amount of help required to achieve the desired result.

What is required from each stakeholder?

Consider the level of support required from each stakeholder and the roles they are required to play. What actions are they required to perform? This might involve the reinforcement of training outcomes – for example, a video from senior leaders stating that this improvement initiative is important.

What messages should be conveyed?

Identify the message each stakeholder needs so that they are persuaded to support and engage with the improvement initiative. These messages typically demonstrate the benefit of the initiative to the person or organization, and will focus on key performance drivers such as increasing profitability or delivering real improvements. Messages need to include negative consequences; being transparent increases credibility and consolidates the relationship with stakeholders.

Identify actions and communications

Identify what message or action will win and manage the support of each stakeholder, including the most appropriate channel of communication with the stakeholder.

Focusing on the high-power/high-interest stakeholders first and the low-interest/low-power stakeholders last, devise a practical plan to communicate with each one, including the appropriate amount of information for each stakeholder. Be careful not to over-communicate or under-communicate.

Consider what can be done to keep the initiative's best supporters engaged and on board. Think about how to win over or neutralize opposition. Where the active support of people who are not currently interested in the initiative is required, devise a plan for how to engage them and raise their level of interest.

Consider how these actions will affect the stakeholders. Inform people as early as possible of difficult issues that may arise, and discuss with them how to minimize or manage the impact.

The next step is to implement the stakeholder plan. As with all plans, it will be easier to break it down into a series of small achievable steps, to be implemented one by one.

Toolkit

Section 7.4.3 contains a stakeholder communication plan template.

6.6.3 Sponsor management

Sponsorship is critical to the success of an improvement initiative. The level and extent of the sponsorship will depend on the size and scope of the improvement. When an organization is resistant to improvement and change, a higher level of support and sponsorship is required. Smaller improvement initiatives within organizations that embrace change require less sponsorship.

Tip

A sponsor denotes a manager or business leader required to advocate for a change and who is in a position to authorize that change.

For a medium to large improvement initiative, a coalition of sponsors, led by an authorizing sponsor, is required to support the initiative and manage any resistance to the change. Sponsors must be visible to those impacted by the improvement and, along with middle managers and front-line supervisors, will be responsible for communicating with employees. Small improvement initiatives may only require one sponsor.

A sponsor diagram identifies the required sponsors and the impacted groups, who fall into one of the following three groups:

● **Authorizing sponsor** Authorizes, legitimizes and demonstrates ownership of the change, and possesses sufficient organizational power and/or influence to initiate resource commitment. The authorizing sponsor could be the CEO, CIO or a team leader, depending on the impacted target group(s)

● **Reinforcing sponsor** Reinforces the change at the local level

● **Target (impacted) group** These are the individuals and/or teams impacted by the change.

Toolkit

For more information about sponsor diagrams, including an example (Figure 7.5), see section 7.4.4.

Sponsor commitment needs to cascade down to all affected levels of the organization.

Note that if another improvement initiative is underway within your organization that aligns with your own initiative, consider leveraging the sponsorship of the other initiative.

Having created the sponsor diagram, the next step is to produce a sponsor plan or roadmap that maps out the roles and responsibilities of each sponsor throughout the initiative. Activities and phases can be added or removed depending on the nature of the initiative – for example, to include planning, transition and post-implementation phases.

Toolkit

An example of a sponsor roadmap is included in section 7.4.5.

6.6.4 Communication

Communication is a critical component of any improvement initiative and OCM cannot be managed without it. Communication allows messages to be disseminated about the change, including:

● The current situation and the reason for change

● A vision of how things will look after the change

● What is changing, how it will change and when

● The expectation that change will happen and is not a choice

● Status updates on the implementation of the change, including success stories.

It also allows dissemination of information about how the change will impact individuals, including:

● The impact of the change on day-to-day activities of individuals (WIIFM – What's in it for me?)

● Specific behaviours and activities expected from individuals including support of the change

● Ways in which individuals can get more information, support and assistance in relation to the change.

See Chapter 5 for further information on communication.

6.6.4.1 Monitor effectiveness

Communication is a two-way process. It is important to gather feedback regarding the effectiveness of each mode of communication by:

- asking people from different audiences how they think it is going
- checking that they understand the messages they need to hear
- asking line management whether they believe their staff have understood the messages.

Monitoring feedback on your communication approach is a vital way to ascertain whether the improvement is being adopted as intended, and it allows an opportunity to fine-tune future communications to better meet the needs of the audience and address any gaps.

6.6.5 Empowerment

John Kotter believed that empowerment through broad-based action was a fundamental component of a successful improvement initiative. As such, obstacles that block the initiative or disempower individuals with unrealistic and unattainable goals must be addressed. Supervisors, subordinates, information systems, or even a lack of knowledge or skills, can act as barriers to progress.

With the assistance of sponsors and with continuing communication with other organizational stakeholders, barriers that hinder the change effort can be identified and eliminated. Organizational processes, clear roles and responsibilities, procedures and reward systems will need to be aligned with the desired future state.

Empowerment also involves investment in training. Providing training not only positions an individual to better support the improvement initiative, but it is also in the best interest of the employee.

Key message

Structured training programmes in a service management initiative will provide many benefits, in addition to skills and competence development:

- Speed up the time to realize the intended benefits of the initiative and maximize the chance of overall success
- Create overall awareness and understanding of the ITIL framework and terminology
- Provide a platform where the relevance of the new learning for the organization can be discussed in groups
- Highlight skills and competence deficiencies so that additional skills and competence development initiatives can be taken, such as coaching and soft-skills development
- Provide a pool of process-trained resources.

6.6.5.1 Groundwork for training

It is critical that the new behaviour, attitudes and skills that managers and employees need are identified and a plan is formed to determine how to provide them. Before defining a detailed training plan, it is important to understand the problems that the training is intended to solve:

- What are the desired behaviours that need to change?
- What are the learning objectives?

It is also important to scope and manage the return on value of a learning intervention or training initiative. The eight-field model can be used to achieve this. The model sets out to answer two key questions:

● What do we want to achieve?

● How can we evaluate that we achieved what we set out to realize?

Toolkit

A description of the eight-field model is included in section 7.4.9.

6.6.5.2 Training needs analysis

Having understood the desired behaviours and skills required, a training needs analysis (TNA) can be conducted to determine areas of weakness. The TNA can be undertaken by interview, survey, observation, examination of training records etc.

Once the areas of weakness have been identified, a training plan can be created which includes a matrix of who requires training, and in what area.

Example

An organization implemented automated fulfilment options connected to their service request catalogue. The goal was to reduce the number of calls to the service desk for service requests such as approved application installations, laptop requests, hardware and software faults. These requests would be sent directly to the appropriate fulfilment team.

Six months after the implementation, calls to the service desk had not reduced in line with expectations. An investigation determined that end-users could not easily find what they were looking for through the service request catalogue and therefore reverted to calling the service desk.

An improvement initiative was instigated to restructure the service request catalogue and its interfaces, in order to make it much more user-friendly. The initiative also improved the service catalogue process. Supporting technology was changed to support the process change.

Table 6.4 shows the TNA matrix.

Table 6.4 Example of a training needs analysis matrix

Team	Training needs analysis			
	New look and feel navigation	Technology	New process overview	In-depth process training
Service desk	X	X	X	
End-user	X			
Process managers				X
Fulfilment teams		X	X	
Senior management			X	

6.6.5.3 Training methods

Various training methods are available including:

- External training courses
- Internal training courses
- Experiential learning (for example, simulations)
- Programmed learning (for example, computer-based learning)
- Tutorial
- On-the-job training
- Coaching and mentoring
- Video.

The needs of the individual should determine the most appropriate training method.

6.6.5.4 Timing

A useful technique for determining the most appropriate date for the training is to work back from the planned implementation date. It should not take place too early or the trainee may forget what they have learned by the time the implementation takes place. It should not be so close to the implementation date that the trainee does not have time to absorb the learning or have an opportunity to ask questions.

If the trainee is to be provided with an acceptance test environment or a sandbox, in order to familiarize themselves with the changed technology before they go live, their training should be delivered prior to being given access to the live technology.

6.6.5.5 Training plan

A training plan, an example of which is shown in Table 6.5, can be devised to reflect the TNA, the way in which the training will be delivered (which may utilize a combination of approaches) and the timing of the training. The plan should include measures by which to determine that the training is functioning – that is, having the desired effect.

Toolkit

A training plan template is included in section 7.4.10.

6.6.6 Resistance management

However beneficial the improvement initiative will be, it is highly likely that there will be resistance to the change. It is important to plan to manage it.

6.6.6.1 Why do people resist change?

The biggest reason people resist change is fear of the unknown. People will only move towards the future state once they believe, or more importantly feel, that the risk of staying in the current state is greater than the risk of moving forward.

Table 6.5 Example training plan for self-service password reset tool

Audience	Content	Delivery	Duration	Dates	Measurement/functioning
Employees	How to use the self-service password reset tool	Video on intranet (embed link in email)	10 minutes	February – March	Increase in uptake of self-service password reset tool and reduced calls to the service desk
Middle managers	How to use the self-service password reset tool	Video on intranet (directions in newsletter) and shown in team meeting	10 minutes	February – March	Increase in uptake of self-service password reset tool and reduced calls to the service desk
Divisional heads	How to use the self-service password reset tool	Video on intranet (embed link in email) and shown in team meeting	10 minutes	February – March	Increase in uptake of self-service password reset tool and reduced calls to the service desk
Service desk	Project plan Timeframes How the self-service password reset tool works How to handle calls to the service desk for password resets (scripts)	Face-to-face (to be recorded for ongoing training)	1/2 day	Every Monday afternoon throughout February	Service desk call monitoring Manager evaluation of understanding Increase in uptake of self-service password reset tool and reduced calls to the service desk
		Edited face-to-face training video	1 hour	Available throughout March	Service desk call monitoring Manager evaluation of understanding Increase in uptake of self-service password reset tool and reduced calls to the service desk

People may not have a clear picture of what the change will look like and why it is being undertaken. If they do not understand the need for the change, they will resist it; this is especially true of people who believe that the status quo is the only way things can be done.

If past change initiatives failed or were poorly managed, there may be a lack of trust that this improvement can be effectively implemented. If the benefits and rewards are not seen as adequate when compared with the effort required to make the change, there will be resistance.

If employees have experienced a lot of change within the organization, they may be suffering from change fatigue.

6.6.6.2 Identify resistance

The emotional responses to change models, described in section 6.5, can help determine where people are on the change journey. Actions to determine how to help people transition through to acceptance stages include:

● Provide safe feedback channels for employees to provide comments on the improvement initiative. This could be via email, social media channels or in response to a survey. Make sure this happens early in the initiative to identify resistance and take action accordingly.

● Listen to what people are saying around the workplace and understand their objections. This can happen in formal contexts such as team meetings and targeted interviews, or in informal situations such as conversations around the water cooler.

● Talk to line managers and sponsors to obtain feedback as to where they believe resistance is coming from.

- Ask questions. These may include:
  - Do you know why we are making this change?
  - Do you support the change?
  - Do you have the training and/or support you need with regard to this change?
- Be aware of people saying yes but meaning no. Through observation of behaviour, identify the people who claim that they agree with the change, but who find it hard to make the transition.
- Conduct a game-based workshop to identify resistance in a non-threatening way.
- Run an analysis of attitude, behaviour and culture (ABC) to find out which consequences sustain current behaviour and prevent the acceptance of new/changed behaviour.

Toolkit

Kurt Lewin's force field analysis is a powerful tool to help analyse the aspects of the improvement initiative that may lead to resistance. Details of how to conduct a force field analysis are included in section 7.4.11. Information about attitudes, behaviour and culture (ABC) can be found in section 7.4.7.

6.6.6.3 Managing resistance

Having identified resistance to the change, there are various tactics that can be used to overcome the resistance, including:

- Deliver targeted communication that addresses the 'What's in it for me?' question.
- Provide responses to frequently asked questions (FAQs) and make them widely and easily available. Keep updating the responses as more questions are asked.
- Provide education and training to raise awareness of the need to change and equip people with the necessary knowledge, skills and capability to do so.
- Involve employees in the improvement initiative. Involved employees are more likely to buy into the change than oppose it.
- Be open and honest.
- Having understood objections to the change, remove the barriers wherever possible. A barrier may include an employee believing they do not have the right skills to make the change, which can be addressed through education and training.
- Storytelling can be a powerful tool that can explain the benefits of the change in real and tangible ways. Tell stories about the benefits other organizations have realized through a similar improvement initiative. Talk about previous successful improvement initiatives similar to this one.
- If the resistance is due to change fatigue, prioritize the improvement against other changes taking place.
- Provide sponsors and line managers with the right messaging and tools to help them lead their people through the change.
- Create and communicate quick wins. Invite customers and users to tell success stories about ITSM improvement initiatives.
- Provide support and channels where people can get more information about the improvement. When information is hard to come by and employees feel there is little support, they will resist the change.

Toolkit

The structure and sample content of a resistance management plan is included in section 7.4.12.

Tip

Resistance is not always necessarily negative. Someone saying 'the procedure is stupid and will never work' is negative resistance. However, someone saying 'I don't understand why they decided to design the procedure that way – surely they could have ....' indicates a positive resistance and a mind-set for seeking solutions.

People resisting and offering alternative solutions should be asked to perform a more formal role in the design and/or review process for the improvement initiative and can often become champions and sponsors within their own team.

6.6.7 Reinforcement

It is important to follow up with those impacted by the improvement to check that employees have not reverted to the old ways of working and that the desired state is still being maintained. This is called institutionalizing the change.

6.6.7.1 Feedback and metrics

Feedback from people affected by the improvement is needed to determine the appropriate reinforcement tactics. The feedback may take many forms:

● Feedback can be sought via team meetings, surveys, social media channels, intranet forms, or water cooler discussions.

● Managers can be asked about their staff's attitude in relation to the improvement.

● The change curve (and other emotional responses to change models) can be used as a tool to determine where people feel they are in relation to the initiative – for example, are they still resistant or are they advocates?

● Metrics and performance reports can be consulted to determine whether the target groups are complying with the new way of working.

● The continual service improvement (CSI) register, discussed in Chapter 3, could be used to answer the question 'Was the change fit for use and fit for purpose?' The responses can be analysed to determine candidates for future improvements.

Tip

Ensure that all feedback gets a response, or the next time you ask, people may be reluctant to provide feedback.

6.6.7.2 Actions

Once the feedback has been gathered, it can be analysed to highlight trends or gaps where reinforcement activity should be focused.

Where resistance is apparent, resistance management techniques within a resistance management plan can be reintroduced to reinforce the need for change – for example, storytelling that reinforces the improvement benefits in a clear and tangible way.

Communication can also play a key part in reinforcement. Announcing that 80% of the workforce has now adopted the new way of working can encourage others to do the same.

Making it harder to follow the old ways of working and easier to adopt the new can also reinforce the improvement.

> ### Example
>
> An organization introduced a self-service password reset tool. Metrics showed that initial uptake was slow as the entrenched habit was to call the service desk.
>
> The OCM team took two approaches:
>
> ● First, they made it harder to use the service desk. The interactive voice response (IVR) option on the telephone for a password reset was moved to last on the list, so the caller had to wait longer on the telephone to reach that option.
>
> ● Second, the service desk continually asked callers why they were not using the self-service tool in order to encourage registration and usage.
>
> As uptake started to rise, communication was sent out in the form of posters that said '2,500 of your colleagues are now saving time by using the self-service password reset tool. Are you?' Uptake increased by 75%.

Reward and recognition is a strong reinforcement technique. Reward and recognition for those embracing the change will have a sizeable influence on those who are still resisting the change and will act as a catalyst for them to embrace the change.

6.7 CONTINUAL IMPROVEMENT OF ORGANIZATIONAL CHANGE MANAGEMENT

OCM should be subject to continual service improvement (CSI). The process, activities and techniques employed should all be examined to determine where improvements could be made.

Guidance on the application of CSI is provided in Chapter 3: this can help to identify areas for improvement, utilizing a sense of urgency, stakeholder management, sponsor management, communication, empowerment, resistance management and reinforcement.

7

Toolkit

This chapter covers:
- CSI approach
- Metrics and measurement
- Communication
- Organizational change management

7 Toolkit

The ITIL Practitioner toolkit is a collection of worksheets, assessments, templates and a bibliography, which will be of assistance when adapting ITIL into everyday work practices. Many of these tools are discussed in the preceding chapters and are intended to be modified as you or your organization see fit.

7.1 CSI APPROACH

7.1.1 CSI register

The continual service improvement (CSI) register is discussed in section 3.1.2. It is based on information in *ITIL Continual Service Improvement*, Appendix B. It will ideally be in place before commencing improvements. Use this to track and manage improvement ideas from identification through to final action.

No.	Date raised	Size (small/ medium/ large)	Timescale (short-/ medium-/ long-term)	Description	Priority (urgent, P1–4)	KPI metric	Justification	Raised by	To be actioned by	Date required by

7.1.2 Orientation worksheet

The orientation worksheet is discussed in section 3.2.1.1. Use the worksheet when commencing your improvement initiative to better understand the context, objectives and boundaries of the improvement.

What is the organizational vision?
What does the organizational vision mean for me?
How am I measured?
Where does my work come from and where does it go?
Who reports to me?

7.1.3 Benefits realization review template

The benefits realization review template is discussed in section 3.2.5.1. Populate the template after the completion of every CSI cycle to determine whether the improvement yielded the expected benefit.

No.	CSF	Accountable team/ individual	Key stakeholders	Baseline value	Expected result	Achieved result	Stakeholder sign-off (Y/N)	Lessons learned	Comments
							Y ☐ N ☐		
							Y ☐ N ☐		
							Y ☐ N ☐		

7.2 METRICS AND MEASUREMENT

7.2.1 CSF worksheet

Critical success factors (CSFs) are discussed in section 4.2. The CSF worksheet can be used to log the properties of each CSF.

CSF description
What goal or objective does this CSF support?
What other CSFs support the same goal or objective?
Who cares about the achievement of this CSF?
What would happen if this CSF were not achieved?
Has this CSF been reliably achieved in the past?
What KPIs support this CSF?
Who agreed that the KPIs really do support the CSF?
What reports include this CSF?

7.2.2 Individual KPI worksheet

Complete the individual **key performance indicator (KPI)** worksheet for every KPI. Use the information to help decide whether to keep the KPI, improve it, or eliminate it. Remember to keep the total number of KPIs as small as possible, as long as you have enough to support the decisions. KPIs are discussed in section 4.2.

KPI description
KPI target
What CSF does this KPI support?
What other KPIs support the same CSF?
Is the KPI specific?   (Could someone who reads this KPI description misunderstand what you are measuring?)
Is the KPI measurable?   (Do you know how this KPI will be measured? How confident are you that the measurement will be reliable?)
Is this KPI achievable?   (Has it been achieved in the past? Is it realistic given the current process maturity?)
Is this KPI relevant?   (Can you explain the relevance of this KPI to the related CSF?)
Is this KPI time-bound?   (What is the time over which this KPI will be measured?)
What positive behaviour will this KPI encourage?
What negative behaviour will this KPI encourage?
Is this a leading or a trailing indicator?
☐ Leading   ☐ Trailing
Is this an inside-out or outside-in KPI?
☐ Inside-out   ☐ Outside-in
Is this a progress, compliance, effectiveness or efficiency KPI?
☐ Progress   ☐ Compliance   ☐ Effectiveness   ☐ Efficiency
Who is interested in the value of this KPI?
What action will be taken dependent on the measured value?   (How will this KPI be used to validate, justify, direct or intervene?)
☐ Validate   ☐ Justify   ☐ Direct   ☐ Intervene

7.2.3 KPI balance checklist

Use this checklist to ensure you have a balance of KPIs across multiple areas. If any area shows an imbalance then review the KPIs in that area to identify opportunities for improvement. KPIs are discussed in section 4.2.

How many CSFs do you have in total?								
How many KPIs do you have in total?								
Least/most KPIs for each CSF?	Least			Most				
	KPI types							
	Leading?	Trailing?	Inside-out?	Outside-in?	Progress?	Compliance?	Effectiveness?	Efficiency?
How many end-to-end service KPIs?								
How many process KPIs?								
How many technology KPIs?								

7.2.4 Report worksheet

Use this worksheet to ensure that every report delivers sufficient value. This is discussed in section 3.2.5.1.

What is the report title?
Who produces the report?
How frequently is the report produced?
Who should read the report? (Do they actually read it?)
What actions are taken as a result of this report? (Ideally specify actions that have been taken)
Is the report used to justify, intervene, validate or direct?
☐ Justify   ☐ Intervene   ☐ Validate   ☐ Direct
Are there metrics in this report which have not resulted in actions over the last 12 months?
☐ Y ☐ N
If yes, which ones?
When did you last ask the people who read this report how useful it is and what could be done to make it more useful?

7.2.5 Assessment criteria

There are many different criteria that could be used as a basis for an assessment. The table below lists some of these sources which can be used for criteria, but there are many others that may be considered (see sections 7.4.14 and 7.4.15). Assessment criteria are discussed in section 4.5.2.

Name	Description	Typical applicability
ITIL Maturity Model	A set of about 4,000 questions in 30 questionnaires, covering 26 processes and four functions	Assessments that focus mainly on ITSM processes
ISO/IEC 20000	The international standard for IT service management	Organizations that want to demonstrate compliance to a standard
COBIT Process Assessment Model	An assessment against COBIT 5 using ISO/IEC 15504 (the international standard for IT process assessment)	Organizations that use COBIT as a basis for governance and management of IT
CMMI-SVC	Capability maturity model for services from the CMMI® Institute	Organizations that want to focus an assessment on process maturity, and organizations that use CMMI for software development assessments
AXELOS skills framework	A skills framework that covers project and programme management, IT service management, leadership and personal management	Assessments that focus on skills and competence of staff involved in IT service management or project and programme management
SFIA	Skills framework for the Information Age – a UK framework that can be used to assess the capabilities of IT staff	Assessments that focus on skills and competence of staff, especially in the UK
European e-Competence Framework	A European competence framework that can be used for assessing IT staff capabilities	Assessments that focus on skills and competence of staff, especially in Europe
Proprietary assessment criteria from an external consultant or vendor	An assessment where the proprietary criteria match your needs	

The assessment can be based on one of these criteria, or on a limited sub-set if that is more appropriate. It is perfectly reasonable to create a custom assessment using a combination of frameworks from the following list:

● ITIL Maturity Model: https://www.axelos.com/best-practice-solutions/itil/itil-maturity-model

● ISO/IEC 20000: http://www.iso.org/iso/catalogue_detail?csnumber=51986

● COBIT Process Assessment Model: http://www.isaca.org/COBIT/Pages/COBIT-5-PAM.aspx

● CMMI-SVC: http://sei.cmu.edu/reports/10tr034.pdf

● AXELOS skills framework: https://www.axelos.com/professional-development/what-is-the-professional-development-programme/axelos-skills-framework-and-tools

● SFIA: http://www.sfia-online.org/en

● European e-Competence Framework: http://www.ecompetences.eu/

7.2.6 Assessment report content examples

There are many different outputs that may be wanted in an assessment report, but typically these will include one or more of the following:

● A process metrics graph

● An SLA monitoring chart

● A process maturity scale

● A gap analysis

● An assessment planning worksheet.

7.2.6.1 Process metrics graph

Figure 7.1 is an example of a graph which shows the achievement of the assessed processes mapped against a benchmark. Process metrics are discussed in section 4.4.1.

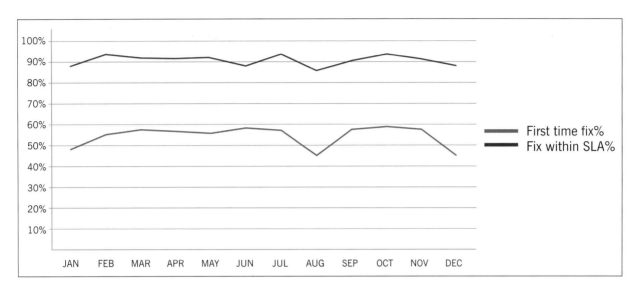

Figure 7.1 Process metrics graph

7.2.6.2 SLA monitoring chart

SLA monitoring (SLAM) shows historical data about SLA targets, often using a simple green/yellow/red coding to allow trends to be easily seen, as shown in Figure 7.2. This form of monitoring is sometimes known as RAG (red, amber, green).

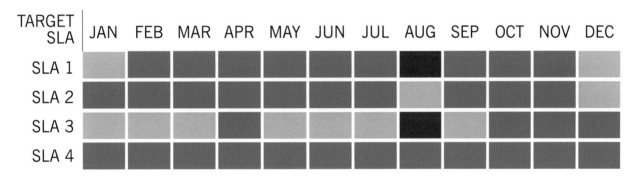

Figure 7.2 An example of an SLA monitoring chart

7.2.6.3 Process maturity scale

Process maturity, as discussed in section 4.5.3, provides an indication of IT service management process maturity as measured against a scale, such as can be seen in the ITIL Maturity Model.

Process maturity, shown in Figure 7.3, is often measured on a scale from 1 to 5 (or 0 to 5). The meaning of the numbers varies, depending on the particular maturity model in use. Typically:

● Level 5 is the highest level of maturity and represents a process that is well managed, is highly efficient and effective, is integrated with other processes and with customer value creation, and is continually being improved.

● Level 1 maturity shows a process that is very informal; it may be achieving the required objectives but does not do so in a way that can be relied on to be consistent.

IT service providers should set their target maturity for each process, based on their needs. It is not usually appropriate to have a target of Level 5 for every process as this could require significant investment without sufficient return.

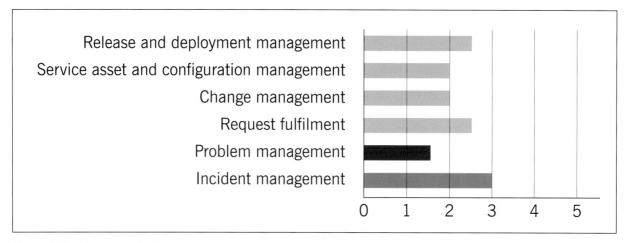

Figure 7.3 Process maturity scale

7.2.6.4 Gap analysis

A gap analysis, as discussed in section 3.2.3.2, lists the required assessment criteria, and provides a summary of whether each criterion has been met and what issues have been identified. The following table is an example of a gap analysis.

	Benchmark objective	Finding	Compliance	Further action
1	There is a documented procedure to record, classify, assess and approve requests for change	The process is documented, but the documentation has not been reviewed for two years and the process followed does not match the documented steps	✗	Contact reviewers to schedule review to get up to date
2	There is a definition of 'emergency change' that has been agreed with the customer	The definition is documented in the process documentation, and both customer and IT staff are familiar with this definition	✔	
3	Decision-making takes into consideration the financial impact of the change	The financial impact of changes is considered by the project office; although this is not part of the 'change management' process it interfaces well and appears to be fit for purpose	✔	
4	...	...		

7.2.6.5 Assessment planning worksheet

The assessment planning worksheet can be used by anybody intending to carry out an assessment. It can be applied to a very small assessment, or to an assessment with a very large scope. In every case, these questions will help to ensure that essential aspects of the assessment have not been missed.

What is the reason for carrying out the assessment?
What action do you expect to take as a result of the assessment?
Who is the sponsor for the assessment?
Who is the audience for the assessment report?
Who will take actions based on the findings of the assessment?
When is the assessment report required?
Who will conduct the assessment?
What criteria will be used for the assessment?
What output do you expect from the assessment (maturity, gap analysis, achievements, benchmark etc.)?
Which services will be in scope?
Which processes will be in scope?
What infrastructure, applications or other configuration items will be in scope?
Which geographies, locations or data centres will be in scope?
Which parts of the organization will be in scope?
Which technical and application support teams will be in scope?
Which suppliers and contracts will be in scope?
Which managers will be interviewed?
Which process or technology practitioners will be interviewed?
Which customers or users will be interviewed?

7.2.7 Tension metrics

Tension metrics, as referenced in section 4.2, is discussed in *ITIL Continual Service Improvement*, section 5.5.2:

The effort from any support team is a balancing act of three elements:

● Resources – people and money
● Functionality – the product or service and its quality
● The schedule.

The delivered product or service therefore represents a balanced trade-off between these three elements. Tension metrics can help create that balance by preventing teams from focusing on just one element – for example, on delivering the product or service on time. If an initiative is being driven primarily towards satisfying a business driver of on-time delivery to the exclusion of other factors, the manager will achieve this aim by flexing the resources and service features in order to meet the delivery schedule. This unbalanced focus will therefore either lead to budget increases or lower product quality. Tension metrics help create a delicate balance between shared goals and delivering a product or service according to business requirements within time and budget. Tension metrics do not, however, conflict with shared goals and values, but rather prevent teams from taking shortcuts and shirking on their assignment. Tension metrics can therefore be seen as a tool to create shared responsibilities between team members with different roles in the service lifecycle.

Example of tension metrics

An organization may focus on increasing the number of incidents handled by each member of the service desk but fail to examine the impact on the resolution rate. If the resolution rate reduces because staff are rushing to deal with more incidents, the overall service quality has been damaged. In this case 'the number of incidents handled per service desk analyst' and 'the incident resolution rate' are the tension metrics that need to be examined together to see the true impact.

7.2.8 COBIT goals cascade

COBIT 5 is a business framework for the governance and management of enterprise IT, maintained and published by ISACA. The following table provides an example of such a cascade. The COBIT goals cascade is discussed in section 4.3.4.

Enterprise goal	Cascades to IT-related goals	Cascades to COBIT 5 processes	Cascades to process metrics
Stakeholder value of business investments	Delivery of IT services in line with business requirements	Manage service requests and incidents	Percentage of incidents resolved within an agreed-on/acceptable period of time
			Percentage of users satisfied with the quality of IT service delivery
			…
		Manage continuity	
		…	
	Alignment of IT and business strategy	Manage enterprise architecture	Level of stakeholder satisfaction with scope of the planned portfolio of programmes and services
			Percentage of IT value drivers mapped to business value drivers
			…
		Manage relationships	
		…	
	…		
Optimization of service delivery costs			
…			

7.3 COMMUNICATION

7.3.1 Regular communications campaign checklist

This example can be used to develop an overall communication approach and to identify that regular activities get done. Section 5.3.3 discusses the different types and approaches to communicating with an initiative's stakeholders.

Task	Owner	Due	Complete
Check receiving media daily for feedback			
Speak with customers			
Escalate issues raised (e.g. to CSI)			
Check for updates on changes/downtime			
Prepare draft message for users			
Meeting to consolidate/check week's communications (from CAB etc.)			
Communicate key issues with peers			
Speak directly with new IT people			
Review all media (intranet/posters/portal/social) for currency of messages			
Send out communications			

7.3.2 Workshop and meeting action plan

This plan can be used as a framework for preparing for meetings. Section 5.3.3 discusses the different communication types and approaches to communicating with an initiative's stakeholders.

Preparation	Notes	Complete
Define objective – tangible outcomes. For example: ● Commence initiative ● Issue resolution ● Process/functional definition ● Awareness and consensus ● Agreement ● Momentum ● Review and action plan		
Scope content (high level): ● Content – presentation/discussion/breakout/creating content ● Agenda – timings/breaks ● Principles/rules of engagement – are there specific constraints or methods that need to be employed?		
Define attendees: ● Essential ● Important for influence/guidance/PR ● Important for inclusion		
Review non-invitees – identify mitigation/explanation		
Identify appropriate workshop facilitator and brief with scope etc.		

Workshop and meeting action plan continues

Preparation *continued*	Notes	Complete
Book room and invite attendees: ● Check for key attendees' availability ● Identify the best means to contact – email or talk first?		
Prepare detailed content ● Presentation ● Handouts ● Advance reading/papers (in draft) ● Workshop/meeting props – cards/games/forms		
Review and chase attendees: ● Check receipts of invitation ● Follow up/socialize/have conversations ● Adjust and accommodate to ensure value ● Be proactive – it is your meeting, make it happen		
Finalize logistics: ● Coffee/lunch ● Flip charts/pens/post-its ● Projector ● Video-chat and dial-in technology – test ● Check the room		
Workshop/meeting		
Allocate summary note taker if possible		
Identify objectives and clear timeframe as per agenda		
Ensure that introductions take place around the room		
Facilitator: ● Ensure that all attendees have their say as much as possible – use breakouts as more opportunity for discussion ● Keep to the agenda and timings ● Keep the session from degenerating into too much detail or specific issues – note issues and concerns, and set these for other sessions ● Summarize the key points discussed and agreed, plus those not agreed ● Clearly define next actions, before thanking attendees on close		
Publish thank you and summary action points within 48 hours		
Build longer-term documentation – merging your initial pre-workshop draft with content from workshop		
Review		
Review checklist: ● Were objectives met? ● What was successful? ● What could have gone better? ● Identify actions and update (this) checklist		

7.3.3 Meeting notes template

The meeting notes template below can be used by a meeting organizer as a framework for creating summary notes, which can be provided swiftly for review after the meeting. It can also be used as a rolling agenda to review actions and progress from previous meetings.

Organizations vary in the level of detail captured in meeting notes. Simplicity works best to keep the focus on key issues and to ensure the notes are actually written and circulated – the more information required, the longer the notes will take to write up, the more chance the notes will disappear down a to-do list. A Lean approach generally works well for most meetings. Section 5.3.3 discusses the different types and approaches to communicating with an initiative's stakeholders.

Meeting title	
Date	
Purpose of meeting	
Attendees	
Organizer	
Work completed this period	
Actions outstanding	
Work next period	
Points raised	
Actions and owners	
Next meeting date	

7.3.4 Business case

The following definition of a business case is taken from *Managing Successful Programmes*, Appendix A.4.6.

[A business case is] used to validate the initiation of the programme and the ongoing viability of the programme.

Typical content:

● The strategic objectives for the programme [or any other initiative], reflecting the vision statement and aligning with the organizational context and business environment

● The expected benefits, with recognition of the organization's ability to achieve the necessary transformation and change

● The overall risk profile, indicating the major risks to programme delivery and benefits realization; detailed risk assessment will be part of the programme's risk register

● Estimated costs and overall timescales; detailed scheduling of programme milestones will be part of the programme plan

● Investment appraisal

● Forecasts of cash flow and expenditure over the programme timeline

● Options and approaches that have been considered, including likely costs, benefits and risks.

Section 5.3.3 discusses the different types and approaches to communicating with an initiative's stakeholders. Additional information about business cases and their role in IT service management (ITSM) can be found in *ITIL Service Strategy*, section 3.6.

7.3.4.1 Business case worksheet

Points for consideration	Outcome
What business challenge do we want to address? In simple terms, how has the issue manifested?	
What should we do? For example, conduct a simple overview (e.g. buy and implement software; hire three new people)	
What business outcomes will this deliver? For example, improve service, reduce cost, manage risk, achieve compliance	
What will be the value of this? For example, it will identify benefits such as improved service quality and reduction in downtime	
What risk will this mitigate? For example, what is the impact of not doing this?	
What work has been done to date? For example, summary of activity, planning, who has contributed/supported, customers, sponsors	
How does this fit with current plans? Identify other corporate strategies that this relates to, and relative priorities	
What is the capital cost? For example, feasibility, procurement, purchase, implementation, training, consultancy, legal	
What will be the recurring costs? For example, 1, 3, 5 years, licensing, upgrades, training and consultancy	
Return on investment (ROI) Year 1, year 2, year 3 – time to recover payment	
Net present value (NPV) Estimate of the present value of the whole investment, assuming expected returns	
What other options are available, if this is not approved? Simple notes to reinforce criticality plus some thoughts on alternative options	
Notes	

7.3.5 Communication success criteria worksheet

Section 5.3.3 discusses the different types and approaches to communicating with an initiative's stakeholders.

What outcome was being sought?
What messages needed to be exchanged?
Who was communication successful with?
Why did that communication work?
What channels worked/did not work?
With whom did we not succeed?
Why did that communication not work?
What would we do differently?
Five key learning points for the future
Notes

7.4 ORGANIZATIONAL CHANGE MANAGEMENT

7.4.1 Stakeholder analysis worksheet

Stakeholder analysis is performed to log the characteristics of each of the improvement initiative's stakeholders and identify the key people who need to be won over. Stakeholder planning is then used to build the support needed for success.

A stakeholder worksheet will help you describe the specific characteristics of each stakeholder group. For more information about stakeholder management, see section 6.6.2.

Stakeholders (group or individual)	Interest/involvement (How does the initiative impact the stakeholder?)	Power/influence/ impact (on the initiative) (high/ medium/low)	Expectations (What's in it for me?)	Observations/ comments

7.4.2 Stakeholder map (power/interest grid)

The stakeholder map as a power/interest grid can be used to map the influence and involvement of the initiative's stakeholders, making it easy to see which stakeholders are likely to oppose or criticize the initiative, and which stakeholders could be advocates and supporters. This can be aided using colour-coding – for example, advocates and supporters in green, opponents and critics in red, and neutrals in orange.

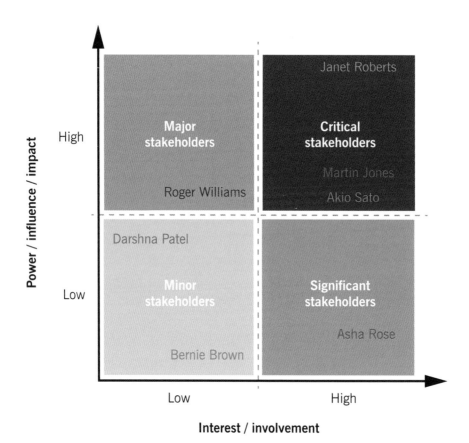

Figure 7.4 An example of a stakeholder map with stakeholders marked

The example in Figure 7.4 is of a stakeholder map for an improvement initiative. It shows that considerable effort needs to be put in to persuade Roger and Asha to become advocates for the initiative. Janet, Martin and Akio also need to be managed closely as powerful advocates. For more information about stakeholder management, see section 6.6.2.

7.4.3 Stakeholder communication plan template

Stakeholder name	Communications approach[a]	Key interests and issues	Current status[b]	Desired support[c]	Desired improvement roles (if any)	Actions desired (if any)	Messages needed	Action and communication
a Critical – manage closely; major – keep satisfied; significant – keep informed; minor – monitor								
b Advocate/supporter/neutral/opponent								
c High/medium/low								

Having conducted a stakeholder analysis, you now have the information you need to plan how to communicate with the stakeholders.

For each stakeholder, complete the stakeholder communication plan using the steps described in section 6.6.2. To summarize:

● Be clear about the overall communication objective. What do you want to achieve, when and why?

● Identify all of your audiences. You can use your sponsor diagram (as described in section 7.4.4) as a starting point.

- Think about the communication objective for that specific audience. For example, do you want them to take action or is it just for awareness? Think about the audience's needs – what do they need to know from you? There may be multiple objectives for each audience.

- Work out the message that will meet your objective.

- Consider what channels you will use to deliver your message, e.g. email, team meetings, posters, intranet, newsletter, bulletin boards, town hall meetings, focus groups etc. Think broadly and be creative; channels other than those normally used within the organization may have considerable impact. Give careful consideration to the preferred channel for each audience.

- Consider from whom the audience wants to hear the message. Employees may prefer to hear about a business-level improvement from a senior business leader, whereas they want to hear about the impact it will have on them from their immediate line manager.

- Consider what questions may be raised as a result of the communication. If appropriate, prepare an FAQ to cover expected questions.

- Work out the timing and frequency of your communication to each audience. Although people do not want to be swamped with communication, key messages may still need to be repeated several times before the communication is fully absorbed. Consider that people may be members of several different groups within the organization, and so may receive the same communication from several sources. Plan so that individuals receive the right information and are not inundated or confused by the different messages they receive.

More information about issues when communicating can be found in Chapter 5.

7.4.4 Sponsor diagram

Sponsorship for the improvement initiative is critical to its success. The level and size of the sponsorship will depend on the size and scope of the improvement. When an organization is resistant to improvement and change, a higher level of support and sponsorship will be required, as opposed to an organization that embraces change.

Sponsor diagrams, such as the one shown in Figure 7.5, can be used to identify sponsors of the improvement.

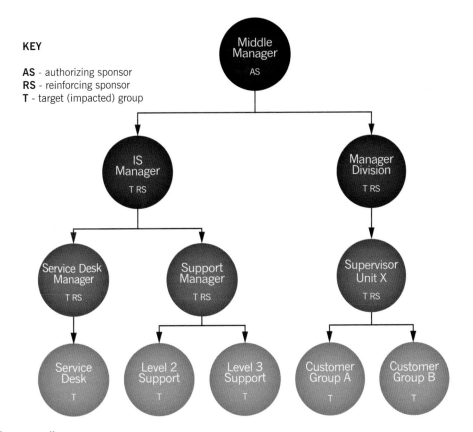

Figure 7.5 Sponsor diagram

To create a sponsor diagram:

● Add the authorizing sponsor

● Add the target (impacted) groups

● From the perspective of the employee, identify who is in charge of the impacted groups and add them to the diagram. Mark those who are reinforcing sponsors – these are the people who are vital for the improvement initiative to succeed.

● Map the key business leaders in between those 'in charge' managers and the authorizing sponsor. Label those who are also a target for the improvement initiative and those who will be required as reinforcing sponsors.

Everything is in place to introduce the improvement initiative to the sponsor coalition in order to obtain their support. Provide the sponsor coalition with the key messages about the improvement and the benefits it will bring. The business case (section 7.3.4) is a good starting point. A sponsor roadmap will be required to map out the roles and responsibilities of each sponsor.

For more information about sponsor diagrams, see section 6.6.3.

7.4.5 Sponsor roadmap

A sponsor roadmap outlines the key roles and responsibilities of each of the sponsors during the improvement initiative. Activities and phases can be added or removed depending on the nature of the intended improvement. For example, the roadmap can be expanded to include planning, transition and post-implementation phases or recreated to align with a more agile approach. For more information about the sponsor roadmap, see section 6.6.3.

Sponsor	Commencement	Design/development	Implementation
Authorizing sponsor	Audience: improvement team		
	Obtain resources for the improvement initiative Provide clear direction Establish commitment to the improvement Be directly involved Remove obstacles Communicate feedback	Stay involved Attend progress meetings Be accessible Remove obstacles Communicate feedback Assist with conflicting priorities	Obtain resources for the implementation Stay engaged Be directly involved Remove obstacles Resolve issues and conflicts
	Audience: sponsors and managers		
	Build a coalition of sponsors and managers to support the change Communicate the business drivers for change and the risk of not changing Provide training on organizational change management for reinforcing sponsors and managers Obtain and listen to management feedback Manage resistance to change	Continue to build support and sponsorship Reinforce key messages Address areas of resistance Support the reinforcing sponsors in managing their transition and that of their employees Keep reinforcing sponsors and managers informed Recognize outstanding reinforcing sponsors and managers Hold reinforcing sponsors and managers accountable Communicate project progress	Continued support Reinforce key messages Address areas of resistance Support the reinforcing sponsors in managing their transition and that of their employees Keep reinforcing sponsors and managers informed Recognize outstanding reinforcing sponsors and managers Hold reinforcing sponsors and managers accountable Celebrate successes

Sponsor	Commencement	Design/development	Implementation
Authorizing sponsor *continued*	**Audience: employees**		
	Share the need for the improvement and how it relates to the organizational direction Share the risks of not changing 'Walk the talk' Repeat key messages over and over Show project milestones and provide progress updates	Reinforce key messages 'Walk the talk' Share project progress Make personal commitment visible	Reinforce key messages 'Walk the talk' Share project progress Make personal commitment visible Look for quick wins and share successes
Reinforcing sponsor	**Audience: employees**		
	Communicate, promote and enforce the change across each employee's part of the organization Answer the question 'What's in it for me?' 'Walk the talk' Repeat key messages over and over Listen to employee feedback and manage resistance to change Tell employees what they can expect to happen and when Coaching and mentoring Provide feedback to improvement team and authorizing sponsor	Communicate, promote and enforce the change across each employee's part of the organization Reinforce key messages Answer the question 'What's in it for me?' Listen to employee feedback and manage resistance to change Recognize and reward the good work employees have done 'Walk the talk' Enable employee participation and involvement in the improvement Make personal commitment visible Coaching and mentoring Provide feedback to improvement team and authorizing sponsor	Reinforce key messages Answer the question 'What's in it for me?' Listen to employee feedback and manage resistance to change Recognize and reward the good work employees have done 'Walk the talk' Celebrate success Reinforcement Make personal commitment visible Coaching and mentoring Provide feedback to improvement team and authorizing sponsor

7.4.6 RACI model authority matrix

RACI tables are a simple way of seeing what level of responsibility each role has. RACI stands for responsible, accountable, consulted and informed. For more information about RACI, see section 6.2.

Activity	Role 1	Role 2	Role 3	Role 4
Activity 1				
Activity 2				
Activity 3				

7.4.7 The ABC of ICT

ABC stands for the attitude, behaviour and culture within IT organizations.

7.4.7.1 Attitude – What people think and feel

When embarking on an ITSM improvement initiative, it is often necessary to change people's attitudes in order to generate buy-in and commitment for the change. Identify and address attitudes that are counter-productive – those that can lead to negative behaviour and threaten the aims of the change programme.

In order to change attitude, it is important to make the attitude conscious and visible, and to relate the relevance of the attitude to the current and desired behaviour. To get people to change attitude, they need to feel negative consequences in relation to the current behaviour and/or see the benefits of the newly desired behaviour.

7.4.7.2 Behaviour – What people do

Behaviour is influenced by attitude and by the culture of the organization, and adopting ITSM or initiating improvement processes requires behaviour to change. As ITSM impacts all levels within an organization – from operational to tactical and line management to strategic managers, as well as the user and the business community – behaviour will need to change to some degree. This is a significant realization because people often do not like to change their behaviour. They may resist in one way or another until they have bought into the benefits of the change. Until that point, their attitude may be one of distrust as well as discomfort, and they may demonstrate a lack of confidence at having to change the way they do things.

7.4.7.3 Culture – Accepted ways of working within an organization

Culture refers to the values and standards that people find normal.

Attitude is individual and comes from personal beliefs and experiences, which in turn influences behaviour. Culture can be described as the organizational or corporate attitude. Often employees in an organization are unaware of the culture and how this influences their personal attitude and behaviour. This is why culture is one of the most difficult things to change. It can stop a change programme in its tracks, and it needs to be taken seriously if the change programme is to succeed.

7.4.8 Balanced diversity – a portfolio approach to organizational change

Many improvement initiatives fail because there is insufficient focus on the activities and practices that need to be carried out in order to embed a change into the organization. Problems such as passive resistance to change, inertia and competing priorities lead to the failure of ITSM improvement initiatives to yield the promised return.

Balanced Diversity (Ferris, 2011) is an invaluable reference guide to overcoming those problems and provides a wide range of practices that every person leading an improvement initiative needs within their toolkit to successfully establish a change into the fabric of the organization.

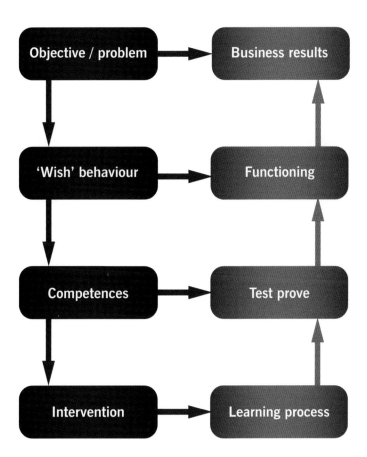

Figure 7.6 The eight-field model

The fundamental difference between this approach and other change models is that it advocates a balanced approach. The practices are arranged into groups of informal and formal practices that either deliver on current commitments (fulfilment) or move the organization further along the path to change (innovation).

The key is to select a balance of practices from each group in order to successfully embed the change into the organization. The framework is structured in such a way that allows practices to be selected from four quadrants. This provides a portfolio approach to organizational change, which includes both formal and informal practices that deliver on current change commitments and which move the organization further along the path to future change initiatives.

It is this diverse yet balanced set of practices that enables change to be successfully embedded into the organizational culture.

7.4.9 The eight-field model – training, planning and management

The eight-field model can be used to help scope and manage the return on value of a learning intervention or training initiative. The model sets out to answer two key questions: 'What do we want to achieve'? and 'How can we evaluate that we achieved what we set out to realize?', which are represented by the left side and right side of Figure 7.6, respectively.

The eight-field model is based upon the *'acht velden'* model' from Kessels *et al.* (1996). The description here uses different terminology and has some additions to the original model. These changes are based upon the findings of using this model with hundreds of ITSM improvement initiatives.

7.4.10 Training plan template

A training plan should reflect the training needs analysis and deliver the specific skills and behaviours that are required for your ITSM improvement initiative to be a success. For more information about training, see section 6.6.5.

Training plan for [improvement initiative name]					
Audience	Content	Delivery	Duration	Dates	Measurement/functioning
Who will receive the training?	What will be the content of the training?	How will the training be delivered (e.g. face-to-face, video)?	How long will it take to complete the training?	When will the training take place?	How will the effectiveness of the training be measured? For example, the service desk is resolving 100% of calls received for account unlocks without recourse to second-level support

7.4.11 Force field analysis

Force field analysis is an organizational change management (OCM) technique that displays and analyses the driving and restraining forces for change, as shown in Figure 7.7.

'An issue is held in balance by the interaction of two opposing sets of forces – those seeking to promote change (driving forces) and those attempting to maintain the status quo (restraining forces)' Kurt Lewin

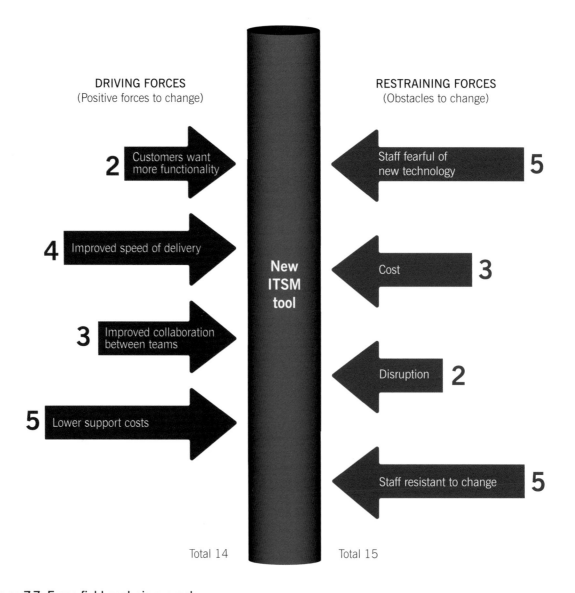

Figure 7.7 Force field analysis example

Created by Kurt Lewin in the 1940s for use in his work as a social psychologist, it can be used to distinguish between the factors that will drive a person towards or away from the desired state. These can then be analysed in order to inform decisions that will make the improvement initiative more acceptable.

Using the template shown in Figure 7.8, you should:

● Describe the improvement initiative or change, and put this in the centre. This should include the goal or the vision of the desired state.

● List the forces *for* the change on the left-hand side and the forces *against* the change on the right-hand side. While doing this, ask the following questions:

  ◉ What business benefit will the change deliver?

  ◉ Who supports the change? Who is against it? Why?

  ◉ How easy will it be to make the change? Do we have enough time and resources to make it work?

  ◉ What costs are involved?

  ◉ What other process will be affected by the change?

  ◉ What are the risks?

● Mark each of the driving and restraining forces from 1 (weak) to 5 (strong). Sum both sides.

● Review the forces and decide which has flexibility for change or could be influenced.

● Create a strategy to strengthen the driving forces and weaken the restraining forces, or, preferably, both. How can the scores of the driving forces be raised, scores of the restraining forces lowered? Referring to the sponsor diagram and sponsor roadmap may help (sections 7.4.4 and 7.4.5).

● Prioritize action steps that will help to achieve the greatest impact. Identify the resources you will need and decide how to implement the action steps.

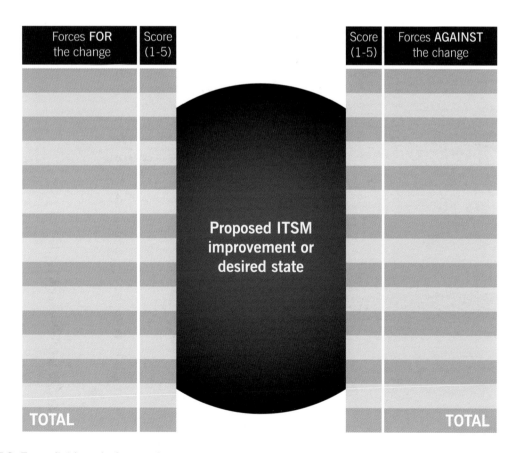

Figure 7.8 Force field analysis template

To help visually, use different-size arrows, as shown in Figure 7.7.

In this example, the strategy to strengthen the driving forces and weaken the restraining forces could be as follows:

- Train staff, raising cost (+1) but decreasing staff fear of new technology (-2)
- Utilize a resistance management plan, raising cost (+1) but decreasing staff resistance to change (-2)
- Demonstrate that change is necessary for business survival (a new driving force: +2).

These changes would swing the balance from 15:14 (against the improvement) to 16:13 (for the improvement). For more information on force field analysis, see section 6.6.6.

7.4.12 Resistance management plan

A resistance management plan is a proactive way to manage resistance to the improvement initiative. The plan should describe tactics for managing resistance at each level of the organization. The levels included will be determined by the nature of the improvement initiative. For more information on resistance management, see section 6.6.6.

Preparation	Notes	Complete

Methods to counter surface resistance:
● Employee feedback. For example:
  ◦ Social media channels
  ◦ Surveys
  ◦ Interviews
  ◦ Email
● Supervisor feedback. For example:
  ◦ Weekly face-to-face meetings
  ◦ Email
● Observation and listening. For example:
  ◦ Observing behaviours and listening to what employees are saying
  ◦ Identifying objections.		

Process for resistance management for each impacted level within the organization.
● Employees. For example:
  ◦ Increased communication
  ◦ Targeted communication at resistant groups
  ◦ Town hall meetings
  ◦ Face-to-face meetings
  ◦ Resistance management training for supervisors and middle management
● Middle management. For example:
  ◦ Face-to-face meetings
  ◦ Team meetings
  ◦ Personal communication from primary/authorizing sponsor
  ◦ Resistance management training for executives
● Executives. For example:
  ◦ Face-to-face meetings
  ◦ Team meetings
  ◦ Personal communication from primary/authorizing sponsor
  ◦ Organizational change management training for executives		

7.4.13 Determine the amount of organizational change management

Every improvement initiative should understand the context of the organization into which the improvement is being implemented. It should also understand the nature of the improvement. Asking questions about these two aspects will bring about this understanding.

The following two assessments – organizational assessment and nature of the ITSM improvement – will help determine how much organizational change effort and resources your ITSM improvement initiative will require (for more information, see Chapter 6).

7.4.13.1 Organizational assessment example

Assess your organization against the questions in the following example. Choose the answer *most* reflective of your organization. Mark your answer as either 1, 2 or 3. Add up the scores.

Question	Score		
	1	2	3
How change resistant is the organization?	Open to change	Partially	Highly resistant to change
How much change is currently taking place?	Large amount of change	Medium amount of change	No change
Were past improvement initiatives seen as positive or negative?	Positive	Partially	Negative
How do management reward people?	For embracing change and risk taking	Somewhere in between	Consistency and maintaining the status quo
Are adequate resources available for improvement initiatives?	Yes	Sometimes	No
Is there is a clear vision for the organization?	Yes	Partially	No
Do we effectively communicate the reason for improvement initiatives throughout the change?	Yes	Partially	No
Do employees understand the need for continual improvement and change?	Yes	Partially	No
Are change agents (those responsible for implementation of the change) highly respected with a successful track record?	Yes	Partially	No
Are sponsors (managers needed to be advocates for the change and authorize it) highly respected with a successful track record?	Yes	Partially	No

Low 1–10 Indicates an organization open and embracing of improvements with an environment and capability to support a successful improvement initiative. The initiative is low in risk from an organizational change management perspective. The need for organizational change management resources and effort will be relatively small.

Medium 11–20 Indicates an organization that is midway between being highly resistant to improvement and change and being open to change. There may be a mixture of capability and perception of past improvement initiatives. Work will need to be done to determine where the pockets of resistance are and OCM plans will be needed to address those pockets of resistance.

High 21–30 Indicates an organization that is highly resistant to change, with a poor history of improvement initiatives and a low organizational change management competency. The organizational change management plans will need to address resistance to change, and more effort and resources will be required from an organizational change management perspective.

7.4.13.2 Nature of the ITSM improvement

Assess your ITSM improvement initiative against the questions in the table. Choose the answer *most* reflective of your organization. Mark your answer as either 1, 2 or 3. Add up the scores.

Question	Score		
	1	2	3
What is the reach of the improvement initiative?	Confined to a small area of the organization (e.g. department)	Medium reach across the organization (e.g. division)	Wide-ranging across the entire organization
Does the improvement bring about a change in processes?	None	Partially	Totally
Does the improvement bring about a change in technology?	None	Partially	Totally
Does the improvement bring about a change in roles?	None	Partially	Totally
Does the improvement mean a change in organizational structure?	None	Partially	Totally
Is this a complex change?	Simple	Partially	Complex
How many employees will be impacted?	10s	100s	1000s
Are all the impacted groups impacted in the same way?	Yes	Partially	No
Can the improvement be aligned with the organizational strategy and vision?	Yes	Partially	No
How long is it going to take to implement the improvement?	Weeks	Months	Years

Low 1–10 Indicates a minimal change, which will require a small amount of OCM.

Medium 11–20 Indicates a medium change, which will require more OCM.

High 21–30 Indicates a large and complex change, which will require a significant amount of OCM.

7.4.14 Frequently adopted OCM frameworks

This section provides further guidance on the more frequently adopted OCM frameworks and approaches.

7.4.14.1 Prosci®

Founded in 1994, Prosci is a world leader in benchmarking research and change management products. Prosci's tools and methodology are based on best-practices research with more than 3,400 international organizations. The Prosci methodology has become one of the most widely used approaches to managing the people side of change in business and government.

Prosci's three-phase change management process comprises:

● Phase 1: Preparing for change

● Phase 2: Managing change

● Phase 3: Reinforcing change.

Prosci reports that projects with excellent organizational change management effectiveness are six times more likely to meet or exceed project objectives.

According to Prosci, the project risks when OCM is not managed effectively are as follows:

● Productivity declines

● Passive resistance escalates

● Active resistance emerges and sabotages the change

● Valued employees leave the organization

- Morale deteriorates
- Projects go over budget and past their deadline
- Employees find workarounds to avoid the new way of doing things or revert to the old way
- Divides are created in the organization between us and them
- The organization builds a history of failed and painful changes.

The Prosci research, *Best Practices in Change Management* (2014), found the greatest contributors to the success of a project were:

- Active and visible executive sponsorship
- Structured organizational change management approach
- Dedicated organizational change management resources and funding
- Frequent and open communication about the change and the need for change
- Employee engagement and participation
- Engagement and integration with project management
- Engagement with and support from middle management.

ADKAR®

The Prosci ADKAR (awareness, desire, knowledge, ability and reinforcement) model addresses the transitions of individuals affected by change with a five-step process that can be used by managers, executives and employees to identify and remove barriers to successful change. ADKAR describes the five key building blocks that form the basis of the Prosci ADKAR model. Individuals make changes successfully when they have the necessary awareness, desire, knowledge, ability and reinforcement.

7.4.14.2 Accelerating implementation methodology (AIM®)

Accelerating implementation methodology (AIM) is the methodology of Implementation Management Associates (IMA). It advocates a 10-step change management approach:

- Define the change
- Build agent capacity
- Assess the climate
- Generate sponsorship
- Determine change approach
- Develop target readiness
- Build communication plan
- Develop reinforcement strategy
- Create cultural fit
- Prioritize action.

7.4.14.3 People-centred implementation (PCI)®

People-centred implementation (PCI) is the methodology from Changefirst and is centred on six CSFs:

- Shared change purpose
- Effective change leadership
- Powerful engagement processes
- Committed local sponsors
- Strong personal connection
- Sustained personal performance.

7.4.14.4 Kurt Lewin's three-step change methodology

Lewin's methodology has three steps:

- **Unfreeze** People and organizations must undergo preparation for change before change can be effected.
- **Change** People who have been unfrozen through driving forces (and the absence of restraining forces) are in a transition that can result in a change of behaviour or procedure that can help them become more effective team members. Organizations that have accepted the driving forces behind change can also be directed into more constructive and profitable business practices.
- **Refreeze** The final stage of the Kurt Lewin change model calls for the new methods, procedures, thought patterns, and behaviours to be cemented into place. New relationships, new procedures, new systems are now in situ and must be accepted in order to make their implementation successful.

7.4.14.5 John Kotter – eight steps in leading change

Kotter's eight steps are:

- Create a sense of urgency
- Form a guiding coalition
- Develop a vision and strategy
- Communicate the vision
- Enable action and removal of obstacles
- Generate short-term wins
- Hold the gains and build on change
- Anchor new approaches in the culture.

7.4.14.6 McKinsey study: helping employees embrace change

This study (LaClair and Rao, 2002) showed that the ROI was 143% when a strong OCM programme was included as part of the initiative and only 35% when there was a weak OCM programme (Figure 7.9).

The 11 most unsuccessful companies in the McKinsey study had poor OCM, which showed the following:

- Lack of commitment and follow-through by senior executives
- Defective project management skills among middle managers
- Lack of training and confusion among front-line employees.

The 11 most successful companies in the study had excellent OCM programmes:

- Senior and middle managers and front-line employees were all involved
- Everyone's responsibilities were clear
- The reasons for the project were understood and accepted throughout the organization.

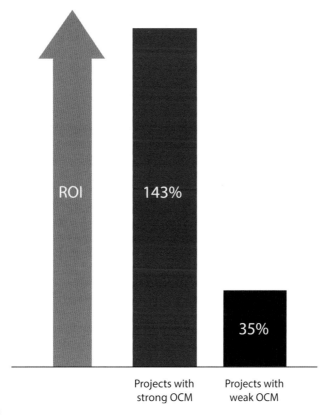

ROI   143%   35%

Projects with
strong OCM

Projects with
weak OCM

Figure 7.9 OCM and ROI

7.4.15 Agile, Kanban, Lean and DevOps

PRINCE2 Agile lists the fundamental values and principles of agile (including the Agile Manifesto). There are a wide variety of agile frameworks, methods and approaches, and many of them promote a set of fundamental behaviours, referred to as 'principles' and 'values'. They represent a mind-set and are usually core to the way an approach works, and therefore if they are compromised then so is the approach.

The values and principles of some of the agile frameworks, methods and approaches are discussed in *PRINCE2 Agile*. Some of the approaches below are for software development only.

7.4.15.1 The Agile Manifesto (The Manifesto for Agile Software Development)

We are uncovering better ways of developing software by doing it and helping others do it. Through this work we have come to value:

- **Individuals and interactions** over processes and tools
- **Working software** over comprehensive documentation
- **Customer collaboration** over contract negotiation
- **Responding to change** over following a plan.

That is, while there is value in the items on the right, we value the items on the left more.

The manifesto is a set of values (http://www.agilemanifesto.org). There are 12 principles behind it:

- Our highest priority is to satisfy the customer through early and continuous delivery of valuable software.
- We welcome changing requirements, even late in development. Agile processes harness change for the customer's competitive advantage.
- We deliver working software frequently, from a couple of weeks to a couple of months, with a preference for the shorter timescale.
- Business people and developers must work together daily throughout the project.

- We build projects around motivated individuals, give them the environment and support they need, and trust them to get the job done.
- The most efficient and effective method of conveying information to and within a development team is face-to-face conversation.
- Working software is the primary measure of progress.
- Agile processes promote sustainable development. The sponsors, developers and users should be able to maintain a constant pace indefinitely.
- Continuous attention to technical excellence and good design enhances agility.
- Simplicity – the art of maximizing the amount of work not done – is essential.
- The best architectures, requirements and designs emerge from self-organizing teams.
- At regular intervals, the team reflects on how to become more effective, then tunes and adjusts its behaviour accordingly.

7.4.15.2 The Kanban method

Kanban is based on four foundational principles:

- Start with what you do now
- Agree to pursue evolutionary change
- Initially, respect current roles, responsibilities and job titles
- Encourage acts of leadership at all levels.

The Kanban method is made up of six core practices:

- Visualize
- Limit **work in progress (WIP)**
- Manage the flow
- Make policies explicit
- Implement feedback loops
- Improve collaboratively.

7.4.15.3 Lean

In Lean, the core idea is to maximize customer value while minimizing waste. Simply, Lean means creating more value for customers with fewer resources.

A Lean organization understands customer value and focuses its key processes to continuously increase it. The ultimate goal is to provide perfect value to the customer through a perfect value creation process that has zero waste.

To accomplish this, Lean thinking changes the focus of management from optimizing separate technologies, **assets**, and vertical departments to optimizing the flow of products and services through entire value streams that flow horizontally across technologies, assets and departments to customers.

Eliminating waste along entire value streams, instead of at isolated points, creates processes that need less human effort, less space, less capital, and less time to make products and services at far less cost and with much fewer defects, compared with traditional business systems. Companies are able to respond to changing customer desires with high variety, high quality, low cost and very fast throughput times. Also, information management becomes much simpler and more accurate.

Lean principles can be summarized as follows:

- Specify the value desired by the customer
- Identify the value stream for each product providing that value, and challenge all of the wasted steps (generally nine out of ten) currently necessary to provide it

- Make the product flow continuously through the remaining value-added steps
- Introduce pull between all steps where continuous flow is possible
- Manage toward perfection so that the number of steps and the amount of time and information needed to serve the customer continually falls.

(Taken from: http://www.lean.org/WhatsLean/)

7.4.15.4 DevOps

DevOps (a portmanteau of development and operations) is a philosophy and a movement focusing on organization-wide collaboration to support the delivery of value to the organization and its customers. The drivers for DevOps can be seen in the increasing awareness and acceptance of the complexity of business and technology environments, the rapid developments within IT that make it possible to 'do the right thing right', and the overall acknowledgement of the crucial role that people play within this and the value that they bring. These aspects are all aligned with the ITSM mind-set.

DevOps focuses on four highly integrated areas, covering values, behaviours, patterns, practices and techniques:

- Culture
- Automation
- Measurement
- Sharing.

The Phoenix Project: A Novel About IT, DevOps, and Helping Your Business Win (Kim *et al.*, 2013) provides a good insight to how the DevOps philosophy can help organizations to overcome challenges with the four focus areas, as well as how this links to 'The Three Ways', the key principles behind DevOps, as coined by Gene Kim:

- Systems thinking
- Amplify feedback loops
- Culture of continual experimentation and learning.

Bibliography

Bibliography

AXELOS PUBLICATIONS

AXELOS (2014). *Portfolio, Programme and Project Management Maturity Model* (P3M3). https://www.axelos.com/best-practice-solutions/p3m3

AXELOS (2015). *PRINCE2 Agile*. The Stationery Office, London.

Cabinet Office (2011). *ITIL Continual Service Improvement*. The Stationery Office, London.

Cabinet Office (2011). *ITIL Service Design*. The Stationery Office, London.

Cabinet Office (2011). *ITIL Service Operation*. The Stationery Office, London.

Cabinet Office (2011). *ITIL Service Strategy*. The Stationery Office, London.

Cabinet Office (2011). *ITIL Service Transition*. The Stationery Office, London.

Cabinet Office (2011). *Management of Portfolios*. The Stationery Office, London.

Cabinet Office (2011). *Managing Successful Programmes*. The Stationery Office, London.

Cabinet Office (2013). *Portfolio, Programme and Project Offices*. The Stationery Office, London.

Dorst, S., Major-Goldsmith, M. and Robinson, S. (2015). Who is the king of SIAM? [online]. AXELOS, London. https://www.axelos.com/case-studies-and-white-papers/an-example-itil-based-model-for-effective-siam [accessed 28 October 2015].

Holland, K. (2015). An example ITIL®-based model for effective service integration and management [online]. AXELOS, London. https://www.axelos.com/case-studies-and-white-papers/an-example-itil-based-model-for-effective-siam [accessed 28 October 2015].

Holland, K. (2015). An introduction to service integration and management and ITIL® [online]. AXELOS, London. https://www.axelos.com/case-studies-and-white-papers/introduction-to-service-integration-management [accessed 28 October 2015].

Office of Government Commerce (2009). *Managing Successful Projects with PRINCE2*. The Stationery Office, London.

Office of Government Commerce (2010). *ITIL V3 Planning to Implement Service Management*. The Stationery Office, London.

Office of Government Commerce (2010). *Management of Value*. The Stationery Office, London.

OTHER PUBLICATIONS

Ashkenas, R. (2011). You can't dictate culture – but you can influence it. *Harvard Business Review*, June.

Bergstra, J. and Burgess, M. (2014). *Promise Theory: Principles and Applications*. xtAxis Press, Norway.

Blank, S. (2010). Perfection by subtraction – the minimum feature set. http://steveblank.com/2010/03/04/perfection-by-subtraction-the-minimum-feature-set/

Bridges, W. (2003). *Managing Transitions*. Nicholas Brealey Publishing.

Ferris, K. (2011). *Balanced Diversity: A Portfolio Approach to Organizational Change*. IT Service Management Forum.

Goldratt, E. and Cox, J. (1992). *The Goal: A Process of Ongoing Improvement*. North River Press.

Greenleaf, R. Servant leadership. https://greenleaf.org/what-is-servant-leadership/ [accessed 26 October 2015].

Hubbard, D. (2014). *How to Measure Anything: Finding the value of 'intangibles' in business* (3rd edition). Wiley.

Kaplan, R. and Norton, D. (1992). The balanced scorecard – measures that drive performance. *Harvard Business Review*, January–February.

Katzenbach, J., Steffen, I, and Kronley, C. (2012). Cultural change that sticks. *Harvard Business Review*, July–August.

Kessels, J., Smit, C. and Keursten, P. (1996). *Het achtvelden instrument.* http://www.kessels-smit.nl/files/Het_acht_velden_instrument_NL_3.pdf

Kim, G., Behr, K. and Spafford, G. (2013). *The Phoenix Project: A Novel About IT, DevOps, and Helping Your Business Win.* IT Revolution Press.

Kirkpatrick, D. and Kirkpatrick, J. (2008). *Evaluating Training Programs.* Berrett-Koehler.

Kotter, J. (1996). *Leading Change.* Harvard Business School Press.

Kübler-Ross, E. (1969). *On Death and Dying.* Simon & Schuster.

LaClair, J. and Rao, R. (2002). Helping employees embrace change. *McKinsey Quarterly*, November.

Prosci (2014). *Best Practices in Change Management.* Prosci.

Rother M. (2009). *Toyota Kata Managing People for Improvement, Adaptiveness and Superior Results.* McGraw-Hill Professional.

Schilt, J. and Wilkinson, P. (2008). *ABC of ICT.* Van Haren Publishing.

Snowden, D. and Boone, M. (2007). A leader's framework for decision making. *Harvard Business Review*, November.

WEBSITES

Agile Manifesto: http://www.agilemanifesto.org [accessed 28 October 2015].

Agile methodology: http://agilemethodology.org [accessed 26 October 2015].

Change management: http://gbr.pepperdine.edu/2010/08/the-business-impact-of-change-management/ [accessed 28 October 2015].

ISACA. COBIT 5 information is available from ISACA: http://www.isaca.org

ITIL Maturity Model: https://www.axelos.com/best-practice-solutions/itil/itil-maturity-model [accessed 26 October 2015].

Kanban: Limiting work in progress: http://kanbantool.com/kanban-wip-limits [accessed 26 October 2015].

Kotter's eight-step process for leading change: http://www.kotterinternational.com

Lean: http://www.lean.org/WhatsLean/ [accessed 28 October 2015].

Lewin, K.: http://www.britannica.com/biography/Kurt-Lewin [accessed 28 October 2015]

McKinsey & Company: http://www.mckinsey.com/ [accessed 28 October 2015].

Project management declaration of interdependence: http://www.pmdoi.org [accessed 28 October 2015].

Prosci: http://www.prosci.com/change-management/why-change-management/

Value stream mapping: http://www.sme.org/Tertiary.aspx?id=30192 [accessed 26 October 2015].

Glossary

Glossary

Most terms in this glossary are taken from the ITIL glossary. Some terms have been taken from the common glossary, and other terms are new for this publication. The complete ITIL and common glossaries are available online at www.axelos.com

agreement

A document that describes a formal understanding between two or more parties. An agreement is not legally binding, unless it forms part of a contract.

asset

Any resource or capability. The assets of a service provider include anything that could contribute to the delivery of a service. Assets can be one of the following types: management, organization, process, knowledge, people, information, applications, infrastructure or financial capital.

balanced scorecard

A management tool developed by Drs Robert Kaplan (Harvard Business School) and David Norton. A balanced scorecard enables a strategy to be broken down into key performance indicators. Performance against the KPIs is used to demonstrate how well the strategy is being achieved. A balanced scorecard has four major areas, each of which has a small number of KPIs. The same four areas are considered at different levels of detail throughout the organization.

baseline

A snapshot that is used as a reference point. Many snapshots may be taken and recorded over time but only some will be used as baselines. For example:

● An ITSM baseline can be used as a starting point to measure the effect of a service improvement plan

● A performance baseline can be used to measure changes in performance over the lifetime of an IT service

● A configuration baseline can be used as part of a back-out plan to enable the IT infrastructure to be restored to a known configuration if a change or release fails.

benchmark

A baseline that is used to compare related data sets as part of a benchmarking exercise. For example, a recent snapshot of a process can be compared to a previous baseline of that process, or a current baseline can be compared to industry data or best practice.

benchmarking

The process responsible for comparing a benchmark with related data sets such as a more recent snapshot, industry data or best practice. The term is also used to mean creating a series of benchmarks over time, and comparing the results to measure progress or improvement.

budget

A list of all the money an organization or business unit plans to receive, and plans to pay out, over a specified period of time.

budgeting

The activity of predicting and controlling the spending of money. Budgeting consists of a periodic negotiation cycle to set future budgets (usually annual) and the day-to-day monitoring and adjusting of current budgets.

business

An overall corporate entity or organization formed of a number of business units. In the context of ITSM, the term includes public sector and not-for-profit organizations, as well as companies. An IT service provider provides IT services to a customer within a business. The IT service provider may be part of the same business as its customer (internal service provider), or part of another business (external service provider).

business case

Justification for a significant item of expenditure. The business case includes information about costs, benefits, options, issues, risks and possible problems.

business impact analysis (BIA)

Business impact analysis is the activity in business continuity management that identifies vital business functions and their dependencies. These dependencies may include suppliers, people, other business processes, IT services etc. Business impact analysis defines the recovery requirements for IT services. These requirements include recovery time objectives, recovery point objectives and minimum service level targets for each IT service.

business relationship management

The process responsible for maintaining a positive relationship with customers. Business relationship management identifies customer needs and ensures that the service provider is able to meet these needs with an appropriate catalogue of services. This process has strong links with service level management.

capability

The ability of an organization, person, process, application, IT service or other configuration item to carry out an activity. Capabilities are intangible assets of an organization.

change

The addition, modification or removal of anything that could have an effect on IT services. The scope should include changes to all architectures, processes, tools, metrics and documentation, as well as changes to IT services and other configuration items.

change evaluation

The process responsible for formal assessment of a new or changed IT service to ensure that risks have been managed and to help determine whether to authorize the change.

change management

The process responsible for controlling the lifecycle of all changes, enabling beneficial changes to be made with minimum disruption to IT services.

cost

The amount of money spent on a specific activity, IT service or business unit. Costs consist of real cost (money), notional cost (such as people's time) and depreciation.

cost benefit analysis

An activity that analyses and compares the costs and the benefits involved in one or more alternative courses of action.

critical success factor (CSF)

Something that must happen if an IT service, process, plan, project or other activity is to succeed. Key performance indicators are used to measure the achievement of each critical success factor. For example, a critical success factor of 'protect IT services when making changes' could be measured by key performance indicators such as 'percentage reduction of unsuccessful changes', 'percentage reduction in changes causing incidents' etc.

CSI register

A database or structured document used to record and manage improvement opportunities throughout their lifecycle.

customer

Someone who buys goods or services. The customer of an IT service provider is the person or group who defines and agrees the service level targets. The term is also sometimes used informally to mean user – for example, 'This is a customer-focused organization.'

direct cost

The cost of providing an IT service which can be allocated in full to a specific customer, cost centre, project etc. For example, the cost of providing non-shared servers or software licences.

effectiveness

A measure of whether the objectives of a process, service or activity have been achieved. An effective process or activity is one that achieves its agreed objectives.

efficiency

A measure of whether the right amount of resource has been used to deliver a process, service or activity. An efficient process achieves its objectives with the minimum amount of time, money, people or other resources.

fit for purpose

The ability to meet an agreed level of utility. Fit for purpose is also used informally to describe a process, configuration item, IT service etc. that is capable of meeting its objectives or service levels. Being fit for purpose requires suitable design, implementation, control and maintenance.

fit for use

The ability to meet an agreed level of warranty. Being fit for use requires suitable design, implementation, control and maintenance.

function

A team or group of people and the tools or other resources they use to carry out one or more processes or activities – for example, the service desk. The term also has two other meanings:

● An intended purpose of a configuration item, person, team, process or IT service. For example, one function of an email service may be to store and forward outgoing mails, while the function of a business process may be to despatch goods to customers.

● To perform the intended purpose correctly, as in 'The computer is functioning.'

gap analysis

An activity that compares two sets of data and identifies the differences. Gap analysis is commonly used to compare a set of requirements with actual delivery.

impact

A measure of the effect of an incident, problem or change on business processes. Impact is often based on how service levels will be affected. Impact and urgency are used to assign priority.

indirect cost

The cost of providing an IT service which cannot be allocated in full to a specific customer – for example, the cost of providing shared servers or software licences. Also known as overhead.

internal customer

A customer who works for the same business as the IT service provider.

internal metric

A metric that is used within the IT service provider to monitor the efficiency, effectiveness or cost effectiveness of the IT service provider's internal processes. Internal metrics are not normally reported to the customer of the IT service.

internal service provider

An IT service provider that is part of the same organization as its customer. An IT service provider may have both internal and external customers.

IT service

A service provided by an IT service provider. An IT service is made up of a combination of information technology, people and processes. A customer-facing IT service directly supports the business processes of one or more customers and its service level targets should be defined in a service level agreement. Other IT services, called supporting services, are not directly used by the business but are required by the service provider to deliver customer-facing services.

IT service management (ITSM)

The implementation and management of quality IT services that meet the needs of the business. IT service management is performed by IT service providers through an appropriate mix of people, process and information technology.

key performance indicator (KPI)

A metric that is used to help manage an IT service, process, plan, project or other activity. Key performance indicators are used to measure the achievement of critical success factors. Many metrics may be measured, but only the most important of these are defined as key performance indicators and used to actively manage and report on the process, IT service or activity. They should be selected to ensure that efficiency, effectiveness and cost effectiveness are all managed.

Management of Risk (M_o_R®)

M_o_R includes all the activities required to identify and control the exposure to risk, which may have an impact on the achievement of an organization's business objectives.

maturity

A measure of the reliability, efficiency and effectiveness of a process, function, organization etc. The most mature processes and functions are formally aligned to business objectives and strategy, and are supported by a framework for continual improvement.

measurement

An individual piece of data about the behaviour of something of interest. For example, the date and time when one disk in RAID array KG1234 failed, or the date and time when normal service was resumed after recovery from that failure.

metric

Something that is measured and reported to help manage a process, IT service or activity.

mission

A short but complete description of the overall purpose and intentions of an organization. It states what is to be achieved, but not how this should be done.

model

A representation of a system, process, IT service, configuration item etc. that is used to help understand or predict future behaviour.

modelling

A technique that is used to predict the future behaviour of a system, process, IT service, configuration item etc. Modelling is commonly used in financial management, capacity management and availability management.

objective

The outcomes required from a process, activity or organization in order to ensure that its purpose will be fulfilled. Objectives are usually expressed as measurable targets. The term is also informally used to mean a requirement.

operational cost

The cost resulting from running the IT services, which often involves repeating payments – for example, staff costs, hardware maintenance and electricity (also known as current expenditure or revenue expenditure).

operational level agreement (OLA)

An agreement between an IT service provider and another part of the same organization. It supports the IT service provider's delivery of IT services to customers and defines the goods or services to be provided and the responsibilities of both parties. For example, there could be an operational level agreement:

● Between the IT service provider and a procurement department to obtain hardware in agreed times
● Between the service desk and a support group to provide incident resolution in agreed times.

organization

A company, legal entity or other institution. The term is sometimes used to refer to any entity that has people, resources and budgets – for example, a project or business unit.

organizational change management

An approach for managing the effect of change on people, which could be because of new business processes, changes in organizational structure or cultural changes within an enterprise. Put simply, OCM addresses the people side of change management.

outcome

The result of carrying out an activity, following a process, or delivering an IT service etc. The term is used to refer to intended results as well as to actual results.

output

A specialist product (the tangible or intangible artefact) that is produced, constructed or created as a result of a planned activity and handed over to a user.

passive monitoring

Monitoring of a configuration item, an IT service or a process that relies on an alert or notification to discover the current status.

performance

A measure of what is achieved or delivered by a system, person, team, process or IT service.

pilot

A limited deployment of an IT service, a release or a process to the live environment. A pilot is used to reduce risk and to gain user feedback and acceptance.

plan

A detailed proposal that describes the activities and resources needed to achieve an objective – for example, a plan to implement a new IT service or process. ISO/IEC 20000 requires a plan for the management of each IT service management process.

policy

Formally documented management expectations and intentions. Policies are used to direct decisions, and to ensure consistent and appropriate development and implementation of processes, standards, roles, activities, IT infrastructure etc.

practice

A way of working, or a way in which work must be done. Practices can include activities, processes, functions, standards and guidelines.

process

A structured set of activities designed to accomplish a specific objective. A process takes one or more defined inputs and turns them into defined outputs. It may include any of the roles, responsibilities, tools and management controls required to reliably deliver the outputs. A process may define policies, standards, guidelines, activities and work instructions if they are needed.

quality

The ability of a product, service or process to provide the intended value. For example, a hardware component can be considered to be of high quality if it performs as expected and delivers the required reliability. Process quality also requires an ability to monitor effectiveness and efficiency, and to improve them if necessary.

quick win

An improvement activity that is expected to provide a return on investment in a short period of time with relatively small cost and effort.

RACI

A model used to help define roles and responsibilities. RACI stands for responsible, accountable, consulted and informed.

reactive monitoring

Monitoring that takes place in response to an event. For example, submitting a batch job when the previous job completes, or logging an incident when an error occurs.

requirement

A formal statement of what is needed – for example, a service level requirement, a project requirement or the required deliverables for a process.

resilience

The ability of an IT service or other configuration item to resist failure or to recover in a timely manner following a failure. For example, an armoured cable will resist failure when put under stress.

return on investment (ROI)

A measurement of the expected benefit of an investment. In the simplest sense, it is the net profit of an investment divided by the net worth of the assets invested.

risk

A possible event that could cause harm or loss, or affect the ability to achieve objectives. A risk is measured by the probability of a threat, the vulnerability of the asset to that threat, and the impact it would have if it occurred. Risk can also be defined as uncertainty of outcome, and can be used in the context of measuring the probability of positive outcomes as well as negative outcomes.

role

A set of responsibilities, activities and authorities assigned to a person or team. A role is defined in a process or function. One person or team may have multiple roles – for example, the roles of configuration manager and change manager may be carried out by a single person. Role is also used to describe the purpose of something or what it is used for.

scalability

The ability of an IT service, process, configuration item etc. to perform its agreed function when the workload or scope changes.

service

A means of delivering value to customers by facilitating outcomes customers want to achieve without the ownership of specific costs and risks. The term 'service' is sometimes used as a synonym for core service, IT service or service package.

service asset

Any resource or capability of a service provider.

service culture

A customer-oriented culture. The major objectives of a service culture are customer satisfaction and helping customers to achieve their business objectives.

service level

Measured and reported achievement against one or more service level targets. The term is sometimes used informally to mean service level target.

service lifecycle

An approach to IT service management that emphasizes the importance of coordination and control across the various functions, processes and systems necessary to manage the full lifecycle of IT services. The service lifecycle approach considers the strategy, design, transition, operation and continual improvement of IT services. Also known as service management lifecycle.

service management

A set of specialized organizational capabilities for providing value to customers in the form of services.

service model

A model that shows how service assets interact with customer assets to create value. Service models describe the structure of a service (how the configuration items fit together) and the dynamics of the service (activities, flow of resources and interactions). A service model can be used as a template or blueprint for multiple services.

service owner

A role responsible for managing one or more services throughout their entire lifecycle. Service owners are instrumental in the development of service strategy and are responsible for the content of the service portfolio.

service portfolio

The complete set of services that is managed by a service provider. The service portfolio is used to manage the entire lifecycle of all services, and includes three categories: service pipeline (proposed or in development), service catalogue (live or available for deployment), and retired services.

service provider

An organization supplying services to one or more internal customers or external customers. Service provider is often used as an abbreviation for IT service provider.

SLAM chart

A service level agreement monitoring chart is used to help monitor and report achievements against service level targets. A SLAM chart is typically colour-coded to show whether each agreed service level target has been met, missed or nearly missed during each of the previous 12 months.

SMART

An acronym for helping to remember that targets in service level agreements and project plans should be specific, measurable, achievable, relevant and time-bound.

stakeholder

A person who has an interest in an organization, project, IT service etc. Stakeholders may be interested in the activities, targets, resources or deliverables. Stakeholders may include customers, partners, employees, shareholders, owners etc.

strategic

The highest of three levels of planning and delivery (strategic, tactical, operational). Strategic activities include objective setting and long-term planning to achieve the overall vision.

strategic asset

Any asset that provides the basis for core competence, distinctive performance or sustainable competitive advantage, or which allows a business unit to participate in business opportunities. Part of service strategy is to identify how IT can be viewed as a strategic asset rather than an internal administrative function.

strategy

A strategic plan designed to achieve defined objectives.

supplier

A third party responsible for supplying goods or services that are required to deliver IT services. Examples of suppliers include commodity hardware and software vendors, network and telecom providers, and outsourcing organizations.

supply chain

The activities in a value chain carried out by suppliers. A supply chain typically involves multiple suppliers, each adding value to the product or service.

tension metrics

A set of related metrics, in which improvements to one metric have a negative effect on another. Tension metrics are designed to ensure that an appropriate balance is achieved.

threat

A threat is anything that might exploit a vulnerability. Any potential cause of an incident can be considered a threat. For example, a fire is a threat that could exploit the vulnerability of flammable floor coverings. This term is commonly used in information security management and IT service continuity management, but also applies to other areas such as problem and availability management.

trend analysis

Analysis of data to identify time-related patterns. Trend analysis is used in problem management to identify common failures or fragile configuration items, and in capacity management as a modelling tool to predict future behaviour. It is also used as a management tool for identifying deficiencies in IT service management processes.

urgency

A measure of how long it will be until an incident, problem or change has a significant impact on the business. For example, a high-impact incident may have low urgency if the impact will not affect the business until the end of the financial year. Impact and urgency are used to assign priority.

use case

A technique used to define required functionality and objectives, and to design tests. Use cases define realistic scenarios that describe interactions between users and an IT service or other system.

user

A person who uses the IT service on a day-to-day basis. Users are distinct from customers, as some customers do not use the IT service directly.

utility

The functionality offered by a product or service to meet a particular need. Utility can be summarized as 'what the service does', and can be used to determine whether a service is able to meet its required outcomes, or is 'fit for purpose'. The business value of an IT service is created by the combination of utility and warranty.

value

The benefits delivered in proportion to the resources put into acquiring them.

value network

A complex set of relationships between two or more groups or organizations. Value is generated through exchange of knowledge, information, goods or services.

vision

A description of what the organization intends to become in the future. A vision is created by senior management and is used to help influence culture and strategic planning.

warranty

Assurance that a product or service will meet agreed requirements. This may be a formal agreement such as a service level agreement or contract, or it may be a marketing message or brand image. Warranty refers to the ability of a service to be available when needed, to provide the required capacity, and to provide the required reliability in terms of continuity and security. Warranty can be summarized as 'how the service is delivered', and can be used to determine whether a service is 'fit for use'. The business value of an IT service is created by the combination of utility and warranty.

work in progress (WIP)

A status that means activities have started but are not yet complete. It is commonly used as a status for incidents, problems, changes etc.

Index

Index